Beat the Street®: Investment Banking Interviews

2nd Edition

WetFeet®

Helping you make smarter career decisions.

WetFeet Inc.

The Folger Building

101 Howard Street

Suite 300

San Francisco, CA 94105

Phone: (415) 284-7900 or 1-800-926-4JOB

Fax: (415) 284-7910

Website: www.wetfeet.com

Beat the Street®: Investment Banking Interviews

ISBN: 1-58207-248-5

Table of Contents

Interview Workbook 99

A Student's Perspective 127

Beat the Street at a Glance

Investment Banking Breakdown

Each of the following areas will typically have a different interview process (you must know which you are applying for!):

- Corporate Finance (CorpFin)
- Sales
- Trading
- Research

The Three Rs to Prepare for Your Interview

- Research—know the industry and the company inside out
- Rehearse—practice for the questions you know you will get
- Review—make sure that you know your finance and accounting tools

The First-Round Interview

- Treat it as a conversation
- Prepare examples from your past that highlight your skills
- Show enthusiasm for the company and the industry

The Second-Round Interview and Beyond

- If you can, get tips from your first-round interviewer
- Play it conservative at social events
- Be polite, courteous, and humble

Final Interviews

- Model your behavior on that of the people you've met from the firm
- Convey why you want to work at the firm, and only that firm
- Make everything in your past relate to I-banking

The Interview Process

- Overview

- The Bottom Line

- The Process

- Alternatives to "The Process"

Overview

Congratulations. You're about to graduate with honors from a top-tier under-graduate or MBA program. Your degree will be in economics or finance and you have been hailed as the best captain the crew/tennis team has ever known. You were president of the debate society, have played the stock market since age three, and read the *Wall Street Journal* cover to cover every morning (starting with the section on "Money & Investing," your favorite). You desperately want to be an investment banker and consider yourself an ideal candidate. Your GPA never once dipped below a 3.6 and you aced every standardized test thrown your way, without so much as a single prep course. You are a natural-born leader. You are well groomed and have never been rejected from anything you have ever applied to. You are a shoo-in at any firm. Right?

Wrong. Unfortunately (or fortunately, if this doesn't quite describe your accomplishments to date), for the first time in your heretofore successful life, all of this is not enough. Have you given thought to how your hand feels when someone shakes it? Or how you would react if an interviewer started to read the paper at the exact moment you entered the room? (And maybe not "Money & Investing," either—maybe the comics or Ann Landers.) Can you do a back-of-the-envelope valuation of a company? Do you know what an investment banker does and why you want to become one? Do you know how to sell your biggest weakness as a strength? Can you differentiate one investment bank from another? If you hesitated and had to think about any of these questions, then you're not ready for your investment banking interview. The key word here is P-R-E-P-A-R-A-T-I-O-N. Kudos on your past accomplishments, but this time they will only get you as far as the well-guarded marble lobby. It will take a lot more to be invited into the elevator bank and upstairs to a cubicle.

That's where WetFeet comes in. This Insider Guide is designed to help you understand and prepare for the investment banking interview process. In researching this guide, we interviewed recruiters at most of the leading investment banking firms, including Bear Stearns, CSFB, Goldman Sachs, JP Morgan Chase, Merrill Lynch, Morgan Stanley, and others. In addition, we surveyed hundreds of people just like you: WetFeet customers who had gone through the investment banking interview process themselves. And we came up with a number of common themes and interview techniques. In this guide we will try to explain the process, and help you prepare to face the situations you're likely to encounter.

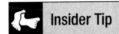 **Insider Tip**

Our number one recommendation? Get ready to sell yourself!

Our number one recommendation? Get ready to sell yourself! Much of banking is really about old-fashioned selling, and the interview process is no different, whether you're seeking an analyst or associate position, and regardless of what area of banking you're pursuing. Interviewers tell us that they will be looking for your enthusiasm for the profession generally and the firm with which you're interviewing specifically (supported by hard facts); your desire to work hard, be challenged, and learn by doing; your confidence in your ability to learn from your unavoidable rookie mistakes; your ability and eagerness to juggle multiple complex projects simultaneously; and your can-do attitude.

While salesmanship is a vital component of all the areas that comprise investment banking, the necessary skills, personality, and day-to-day demands vary dramatically. Thus, it is critical you know the position you want before you start the interview process. Investment banking interviewers possess an uncanny ability to smell blood in the water. You should also know which firm you want to work at and why. To make these determinations, you'll need two things: this WetFeet Insider Guide and a healthy dose of the age-old chestnut, To Thine Own Self Be True (translation for the Shakespeare-challenged: an honest appraisal of what you excel at and what you don't, what types of work environment you thrive in and what types you don't, and above all, whether you can manage the lifestyle—investment banking is a demanding profession, and those who thrive in it are most often people who have put professional success and advancement at the top of their list of priorities).

The Bottom Line

Investment banking interviews are highly competitive. In the end, what will likely set you apart from the rest of the field is your ability to convince interviewers that you are 110 percent committed to being an investment banker, and your ability to demonstrate that you have the skills and personality that will enable you to hit the ground running. Read any firm-specific literature you can find (including, of course, the WetFeet Insider Guides on various investment banks), seek out and talk to friends and alumni in investment banking, and bone up on your finance. And most important of all, stay true to yourself.

The Process

The biggest "feeders" for most investment banks are the undergraduate and MBA programs at top universities around the country. In good years, Goldman, Merrill, Morgan Stanley, and the others each hire scores, if not hundreds, of candidates from these programs. For the most part, the recruiting efforts on campus follow a relatively structured process, outlined below. Moreover, there is surprisingly little variation from firm to firm—most will come on campus in rapid succession. Although firms do occasionally make exceptions, most hire the vast bulk of their campus candidates through the following process. So, if you really want to land one of these jobs, you should start by acquainting yourself with the schedule and making sure that you don't miss that resume dropoff deadline.

Recruiting Season			
	Undergrads	MBA Summer Interns	2nd-Yr. MBAs
Campus Info Sessions	Oct–Nov	Jan	Sept–Oct
Resume Selection	Nov–Jan	Jan–Feb	Oct
First Interviews	Dec–Feb	Jan–Feb	Nov–Dec
Super Saturday	Jan–March	Feb–March	Nov–Jan

Step 1: Campus Information Sessions

These "informal" information sessions are a time to eat well and learn about each firm and its recruiting process. (If your school is not on the tour, the information session at a nearby school may still be open to you. Call and ask permission; you will rarely be told to get lost.) All you have to do is make sure your duds are wrinkle-free, work up an appetite, and show up on time. The recruiters generally bring a current associate or analyst with them. After a brief speech, they open things up for discussion. This is not the moment to impress them with your financial acumen; it's a time to find out how many analysts or associates they're hiring this year, when and how you should sign up for the first round of interviews, who they see as their competition, and how they feel they differ significantly. (Memorize their answers to this last question. Parroting them back, in your own words, at a future interview will gain you points.)

While milling around the food tables afterwards, try to engage an analyst or associate in conversation. He or she is currently in the thick of the job and is therefore one of the best sources of information you could hope for. Even if you find yourself unable to lob a question or two in the analyst's or associate's direction during this time, keep within earshot and listen to the answers he or she provides to other people's questions. Ask for the analyst's or associate's name and work number (get a business card if you can), and whether he or she would mind speaking with you over the phone (which may be necessary if he is she is swarmed by information seekers like yourself). Try to remember any details the analyst or associate divulges. These may come in handy in the interviews ahead.

Step 2: Researching the Job Areas

Still think you want to do this? An important first step in the process is to begin researching the different areas within investment banking and the positions available. We focus here on jobs available for undergrads and MBAs, since these are the slots recruiters must fill by August of each year. Nevertheless, this information is also useful for mid-career candidates seeking to enter at a higher level. Basically, the work falls into four principal areas: corporate finance, sales, trading, and research. Keep in mind: These are very different types of jobs, and most banks won't look kindly upon people who apply for positions in more than one area (the implication being that you don't know what the hell you want to do!).

Corporate finance (aka CorpFin). Corporate finance is an umbrella term for the work involved in capital raising, underwriting, and financial advisory services, including mergers and acquisitions. Every year, corporate finance divisions conduct a formal search for both undergraduates and graduate students, generally MBAs, to fill their training programs.

Undergraduates are hired for two to three years and are assigned the title of analyst (not coincidentally derived from "anal") and graduates are dubbed "associates" (the etymologists are still out on the significance of this word's derivation). Depending on the firm and its needs, an analyst or associate class numbers anywhere from 20 to 90 people. After a brief training in the fundamentals of accounting and finance, analysts are typically assigned to industry groups and from that day on, if they're lucky, they will occasionally sleep, shower, and drop off large piles of clothes at the dry cleaner. The other 80 to 120 hours of the week, they are responsible for gathering data, building and updating computer models, and coordinating production (doing the scut work) for lengthy transaction documents. Associates (the ones with two more years of school under their belts) have the added responsibility of managing a flock of analysts and participating in client relations. They have been hired not just for two interim years, but as "lifers" on the Bank X team.

Mergers and acquisitions (aka M&A). Depending on the bank, M&A may be a separate unit or fall within the corporate finance arena. The work involves advising companies that wish to merge with, or acquire, others. As with CorpFin generally, M&A revolves around the deal of the moment, and can be entirely unpredictable. M&A work is particularly unforgiving in terms of your personal life, given its emphasis on comprehensive quantitative analysis and extensive back and forth with attorneys. The hiring practices vary from bank to bank, but often there are positions for both undergrads and MBAs in these divisions.

Research. Investment banks are "sell side," meaning that the banks are involved in the selling of securities. (This is different from "buy side," which is used to refer to institutions that buy securities, such as mutual funds.) The research departments spend their hours poring over financial data, interviewing people in the industries they cover, writing about specific companies and the economy, and making recommendations about purchasing and selling various financial instruments. Although it sounds academic, investment bankers will tell you that good research is the cornerstone of most any bank's selling franchise: At the end of the day, what the firm is actually "selling" are its ideas (research), which clients pay for through their transaction costs. A limited number of positions in research are available each year. Here, just to confuse the tourists, the nomenclature is reversed: People coming in from college programs are called associates, whereas the stars pulling down seven-figure salaries are called analysts. This is nice work if you like reading (tomes and tomes of reading), a lot of writing (more tomes), plus, just to liven things up, hours and hours of number crunching. Consequently, being a research associate is often solitary work. You already know whether this would suit you. If not . . .

Sales and trading (aka S&T). Sales and trading jobs are split between institutional sales and trading and then broken down further between equity (stocks) and fixed income (bonds). If you want to be a trader, you also have the choice between trading for the firm (proprietary) or for clients.

At most banks, undergraduates and graduates are hired into a training program and then begin a series of rotations around the floor until they find a permanent home. Unlike CorpFin, where your education and title count for a lot, on the sales and trading floor only two things matter: "show me the money," and an ability to swim in ego-infested waters. Hours are driven by the market—when the market on which you sell or trade is in session, you're on. For those of you who are still deciding, you need to know that the trading floor is a poor choice for anyone with genteel sensibilities. For example, it is not unusual to visit the floor on a slow day only to find some sort of binge-eating contest in progress.

With the exception of a few bulge-bracket firms, the recruiting process and training programs for sales and trading (and research) are not as formal as those in investment banking. In sales, you sell. You spend agonizing weeks, sometimes months, "smiling and dialing" your way through the phone book on cold calls to complete strangers. Only the strong survive. One sales and trading recruiter notes, "In investment banking, there are a lot of cooks wanting to get in the brew. There are fewer people pandering to get in here." Traders are perhaps the most wary about whom they hire because any money paid to a junior person comes directly from their pockets.

Because formal recruiting at top-tier schools is not as important a source of fresh S&T blood as in CorpFin, there are typically greater numbers of lesser-pedigreed professionals on the sales and trading floor than in other areas of investment banks. As a result, the sales and trading divisions of many investment banks are divided up into little fiefdoms. At some places, there's a Horatio Alger/Direct-from-the-Mail-Room desk. At others, there's a Bensonhurst desk.

If you weren't born and raised, and if everyone in your family wasn't born and raised, in this part of Brooklyn, you can't work at this desk. Almost everywhere, there's the WASP-wannabe desk. No one here has an Anglo-Saxon last name or a single preppie credential, but until you get very close, you'd swear otherwise. The lords and serfs of these fiefdoms all boast what Ace Greenberg likes to call a PSD degree (Poor, Smart, and a Desperate desire to be rich). (Ace runs Bear Stearns but is still on the trading floor every day.) Of course, there are also plenty of desks where everyone attended Harvard or K-MBA and spent their summers in the Hamptons.

If working in sales or on the trading floor still interests you, be prepared to cover your own expenses to New York for your first interview. Kiss goodbye the fuzzy slippers your classmates interviewing for investment banking are wearing at the Waldorf, and check yourself into the Howard Johnson on Times Square. As you're unwrapping the plastic around the Dixie cups and shutting the blinds to lessen the glare of the lights out the window, keep in mind that in a few short years, when you are leaving your desk at 5 p.m. and your CorpFin colleagues are up till midnight, your bonuses may be large enough to buy your own four-star hotel.

Step 3: Resume Preparation

Okay, now that you know what your life's work will be, it is time to distinguish yourself from your peers with a well-crafted one-page synopsis of your academic, extracurricular, and professional experience. Remember that banking is about selling, and your resume is like a salesperson's "talk sheet"—highlight your strengths and abilities while conveying an obvious predisposition for one of the job areas discussed above. Since the competition officially begins once you drop your resume off at the career center or send it to the firm's headquarters, and since the top banks receive up to 8,000 resumes per season, this is

Career Fairs

We can sum up the notion of one-stop job shopping at a career fair with a familiar phrase: "If it sounds too good to be true, it probably is." The idea that you could give your resume to 100-plus companies in a single meeting place, go home, relax, and wait for calls is a job seeker's pipe dream. Investment banking recruiters acknowledge what you should already have suspected: No one considers a resume submitted at a fair as an official application. A former investment banking analyst who used to regularly represent a firm at career fairs recalls that the recruiter usually trashed all of the resumes she'd collected before she returned to the office. Instead, use the fairs to gather information and your high hopes won't be dashed when you do not receive a call for an interview.

the first hurdle. And it's a tough one. Recruiters will spend anywhere from a few seconds to two minutes assessing your life. Because of the avalanche of paper they receive, they look first for an "instant red flag" which allows them to toss your resume (and aspirations) in the waste bin. (See "Favorite Resume Red Flags" on next page.)

The goal of the resume is to win you a spot on the interview schedule. A current MBA wisely advises: "There are so many aspects of this process that you cannot control, so control what you can. Let them know that you understand the rules of the game." In other words, don't tempt the red flag.

A word to all of you "resume gamblers" out there: Lying or misrepresenting on your resume almost never goes unpunished. Despite the legions of apparently unconnected bankers trawling Wall Street, the Street is in many ways like a small town—people know each other and they love to gossip. Recruiting stories travel like wildfire. Even if you succeed in securing an offer with a false or misleading resume, you may suffer the ignominious fate of having your offer revoked or withdrawn. Don't test the limits—putting a favorable spin on a past accomplishment is entirely different from fabricating one altogether. And don't overstate your verifiable talents. For example, it is not unheard of for someone along the interview chain to see a claim of proficiency in a foreign tongue and choose to conduct the interview in your "second" language. In addition, many firms prepare a resume book of new recruits for distribution firm-wide. Trust us that anything you say on your resume can and will be held against you by your potential colleagues.

 Favorite Resume Red Flags

Misspelled words or grammatically incorrect sentences

Incorrectly spelled firm name (including commas!)

Extremely low GPAs (or one that is noticeably absent)

Any resume or cover letter that is longer than one page

Misstated objectives (e.g., "I want to work for a small firm" in a letter to Merrill)

Bad mail-merges on the cover letter (e.g., a different firm listed on the envelope)

Long-winded sentences

Colored paper and nontraditional fonts

Dos and Don'ts of Resume Preparation

Do

- Copy your resume onto the best white or off-white paper available (100% cotton bond). Many insiders say that they've seen interviewers hold resumes up to the light to check if you are dedicated enough to put your life on Crane paper (with the watermark seal facing text-side up, of course).

- Proofread for both typos and sense. Typos will land you in the garbage before the recruiter has time to process your name. If you are applying to Credit Suisse, remember that while people from Switzerland are referred to as Swiss, the bank is not. Subjects and verbs must agree. Unless universally understood, abbreviations are almost always a bad idea.

- Make the objective on your resume consistent with the firm and the position. Generalists need not apply. The one-size-fits-all job objective consigns you to the clueless file. If you're still uncertain whether your destiny lies in IT consulting or fixed-income trading, design two separate resumes.

- Include items that show off your quantitative skills: relevant coursework, GMAT scores, math SAT scores, spreadsheet and other software you know how to use (e-mail and word-processing do not count).

- Mention without exaggerating, foreign languages you know.

Don't

- Be creative: This is not an artistic profession. Refrain from sending your resume on brightly colored or marble paper, using nontraditional fonts, or hand-delivering a flip-flop with a message about getting your foot in the door. Save all this genius for someone who will appreciate it.

- E-mail the resume: Insiders say that e-mailed resumes frequently do not make it to them in one readable piece.

- Lie about or exaggerate you past experiences.

- Write salary requirements on the resume.

- Write a novel. You are far too young and inexperienced to have a resume longer than one page.

- Show them your pearly whites by submitting a photograph of yourself.

- Lie about your foreign language skills. It is increasingly common for bankers to conduct at least one of your interviews in the language in which you claim fluency.

- Send a sample of your thesis or your current work with your resume. (Unless your thesis or a work project demonstrate particularly well your quantitative/analytical abilities. Even then, brief excerpts will suffice.)

Step 4: The First Interview

The recruiting tour bus arrives on campus to see what the best resumes look and sound like in a suit, under stress, in 30 minutes or less. If your school is not on the tour, your interview will most likely be held at the corporate headquarters. For this first of what you hope will be many "conversations," you should dress for success and be prepared to sell yourself as the ideal investment banking candidate. A human resources recruiter, junior associate, or, sometimes at head-quarters, a mid-level banker will conduct the first interview.

Insiders tell us interviewers are generally looking for you to communicate two points very clearly: (1) why you want to be in investment banking, and (2) why you want a job with this firm in particular. Ultimately, their principal objective is to decide whether or not you are cut out for investment banking at their firm. They deal with numbers all day, every day, so be ready to rattle off your SATs, GMATs (if interviewing for an associate position), and GPA. No need to explain why your math scores lag 22 points behind your verbal unless they ask, though if there are some obvious and odd discrepancies, have plausible, brief answers ready. Do yourself a big favor and do not exaggerate your academic and extracurricular experiences, for more often than not, the recruiter is an alumnus of your university or MBA program and can easily verify or debunk any claims you make. You may find little time to ask questions, but err on the safe side and prepare a few about the firm and the job itself. Make them good questions, not lightweight puffballs—intelligent, careful queries that don't require long answers.

Step 5: "Final" Interviews

Within a day or so you will know if you were loved enough to get an invite to the final round. You have reached star status. Whatever you do, don't let it go to your head this early in the game. "Final" is a bit of a misnomer here; this is merely the filter which separates the capable from the extraordinary. After you receive the coveted telephone invite to the illustrious second round of interviews (often called Super Saturday), you'll be flown to corporate headquarters—or get yourself there by some less glamorous means of transportation—and thrown together with a small army of other hopefuls for a Friday evening of wining and dining and a full Saturday of interviews. (It's not really a "super" way to spend Saturday in their minds either, but this is not the right moment to ask how such a misnomer came into being.)

More than likely the firm will set you up in a posh Manhattan hotel. Don't get too attached to this ornate cable-ready refuge, for you won't be seeing much of it in the next 48 hours.

At this point, the firms assume that everyone assembled is capable of doing the job. Now they're assessing your personality, your behavior in a social and professional context, and whether you are the right "match." This is your moment to emerge from the pack and demonstrate your own unique greatness. We are not suggesting you pull out your favorite party tricks to win over the crowd. Be yourself and stay focused.

On Saturday, you will meet with roughly six or seven bankers of varying seniority for half an hour or more each. Sometimes you'll be grilled one-on-one, other times two-on-one. Here's what they're looking for: how you'd fit in at Bank X; why you want to work at Bank X (instead of equally good, if not better, Banks Y and Z); whether you can crunch numbers accurately and never miss a typo at 2:30 a.m.; and, perhaps most important, the likelihood that you'd accept an offer (bankers don't appreciate having their egos bruised by a recruit's "No, thank you"). Your potential colleagues also want to make sure they wouldn't hate sharing airplane, office, or any other space with you for extended periods, but especially at 2:30 a.m.

Step 6: The Offer and Courting Process

If you've successfully demonstrated your fealty and ability, the phone will ring several days after the final round of interviews. (Some firms conduct third-round interviews, which are typically similar to second rounds, before extending offers). In most cases, it makes sense to remain polite and noncommittal. You will field phone calls from several members of the firm telling you their lives will be empty without you. You'll be invited to a special dinner in New York. There, the firm will give you the hard sell and a date before which they would like you to decide. Enjoy the fame for awhile and then, when you're sure you've found the firm you want to call family (and they will be your only family for the first few years, so you had best be very sure), say "yes" with enthusiasm. If you're lucky enough to have several suitors clamoring for you, say "no" to the rejects with deep reluctance. It's a long life. You never know when you may wish to rekindle their interest.

Alternatives to "The Process"

Not in school? A foreign student? Recruiter doesn't come to your school? You can still get an interview. And you can still get a job in I-banking. Here's what our insiders recommend if you fall into one of these categories.

Midcareer Hires

Bit of a sticky wicket, this one. If you already work on Wall Street, you know where to go—and you're probably not reading this guide. If you're coming from another industry, you'll probably have a tougher time. None of the people we interviewed were willing to describe the "typical" midcareer hires or list the jobs open to them. While everyone is happy to hire lawyers who are fully proficient in banking legalese or people with strong industry experience, and a few firms are usually willing to take a chance on brilliant particle physicists, most tend to fill the gaps in their analyst and associate pools with men and women who have worked in a similar capacity for competitors. If you are a lateral hire, the good news is that you don't have to suffer at your current job waiting out the long recruiting season. Throughout the year, recruiters scurry around to replace those analysts or associates who have either defected or fallen off the corporate track. Because lateral hires are typically not interviewed during the normal training program season, they usually begin their new jobs without much, if any, formal training.

Foreign Students

For those of you with an American undergraduate or MBA degree who want to work for a U.S. investment bank, this is less complicated than you might think, even if your citizenship and visa status (or lack thereof) preclude your working elsewhere. Investment banking is an increasingly global enterprise. Recruiters unanimously agree that candidates who are not U.S. citizens are treated the same as any other applicant; your working status is not an issue. In fact, your proficiency in several languages and close ties to your own country may give you a highly desirable edge. If you receive an offer, the firm will arrange your visa and, after a given number of years, your green card.

Help!

I don't have a prestigious undergraduate degree and/or I attend a second-tier MBA program. Is all hope lost?

No. If the top firms' analysts all appear to be summa econ graduates of *US News & World Report's* Top 10, or if the associate class seems to have been culled from the ranks of former analysts or the Penn and Harvard Clubs, you're not far off. Investment banking firms are disproportionately staffed with Ivy Leaguers and top-tier MBA graduates who get scooped up on the recruiting tour. But there is no need to give up just because the scoop never came for you. There is a way in, albeit a more difficult one. If you're going to be the exception, you need well-honed interviewing tactics. Preparation, strategy, and aggressive but discriminating (not discriminatory) networking will all help get you the job.

The first step is networking. Do not waste postage and precious forest products blindly mailing your resume to every firm. Focus instead on setting up appointments with industry insiders, either through introductions through friends (or friends of friends) or by targeting alumni of your school who work on the Street. Prepare yourself to ask lots of thoughtful, informed questions and demonstrate your commitment to investment banking. Keep in mind that, like the S&T hopefuls, you will likely have to fly yourself to headquarters (most likely New York) on your own nickel (or 8,000 nickels, as the case may be) and pay for your lodging. Don't frown. This show of initiative may just be your ticket in. Remember: Being hungry for an investment banking job is at least as important as having a top-tier school on your resume. What really makes a candidate stand out is enthusiasm and commitment to the work. One recruiter tells us of a candidate she recently hired from a school where the firm does not recruit: "On top of her excellent academic and professional experience, I was so impressed with her initiative to seek out several people in the firm. She demonstrated a genuine interest in investment banking when she flew to New York to meet with us and several other firms over her Thanksgiving break."

Most insiders concede, however, that candidates from lesser-known schools need to have either stellar work experience or fill a unique need at the firm, particularly for CorpFin positions. It also helps if they have previously worked with someone in the firm who can act as a referral. At the same time, several recruiters for sales and trading reveal that they do in fact interview—and hire— many graduates from no-name undergraduate schools or MBA programs. One insider explains that if you went to a lesser known institution you need to be prepared to give a valid reason. The best reason, as you might guess, is that you received a full scholarship (though, as we mentioned above, don't offer such a justification if it isn't true). And if you've already had a lot of relevant experience, the good news is that where you went to school has much less impact on your candidacy.

The Interview Unplugged

- Preparing Yourself for the Beauty Contest

- Research

- Rehearse

- Review

- Investment Banker-Speak

Preparing Yourself for the Beauty Contest

Okay, you've read the brochures, surfed the Web, and talked to alums working on the Street, and you've decided that you want to find your own place in the world of high finance. How can you go about landing one of these jobs? The same way you'd go about doing the job once you're there: with careful preparation and attention to detail. We call this the Three Rs: Research, Rehearse, Review.

Research

The first step in any successful job search is research. Not only do you need to know the positions, you also need to know the players and their distinguishing characteristics. Why? Because, as we've said before, you'll need to convince your interviewer that you are the perfect person for the particular job at his or her particular bank. Your resume, your answers—indeed, your entire persona—must henceforth be steeped in corporate finance (or whatever job area you've carefully selected). And although the jobs within each area tend to be numbingly similar at all the firms, each institution definitely has its own culture and expects its applicants to be aware of this. It is also worth learning the subtle and not so subtle differences amongst the firms so you can be sure to find a good fit.

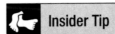
Insider Tip

The first step in any successful job search is research.

For instance, let's say you speak several languages and the international aspects of investment banking are one of your chief reasons for reading this far. Every bank describes itself as "global" these days, but the number of overseas offices, how much revenue these outposts generate, and how many U.S. citizens actually get to work in them are all vital indicators. In fact, the list of firms likely to send you abroad is quite short. If this is really your goal, it will take you less than ten minutes (okay, maybe 30 minutes) to find out everything you need to know from the firm's annual report. If you do this research, you'll not only know which firms offer the best opportunities abroad, but you'll also be able to impress your interviewer with your knowledge of the company's business mix.

If you're concerned about other issues, such as friendliness to women or minorities, you'll have a slightly harder time. How firms treat women and minorities, how much they insist on teamwork, or how much they actually promote and reward "stars" are all sensitive topics. All the recruiting material would have you believe that a harmonious rainbow coalition, the likes of which even Jesse Jackson might smile upon, reigns throughout, from the research cubicles to the trading desks. To collect this information, you'll want to talk to real employees at the firm, read up on them in the press (and WetFeet guides), discuss them on WetFeet.com's discussion boards, and see if they come up in "100 Best" lists (*Fortune*, *Working Woman*). Unfortunately, the reality at many firms is far from the glossy image portrayed by firms' recruiting materials.

Also, be wary of the term "entrepreneurial," which appears frequently in investment banks' self-descriptions. For those of you who have worked with real entrepreneurs, you know that investment banks are about as close to the genuine article as GM is to being a start-up. By "entrepreneurial," investment banks generally mean that individuals are encouraged to shine on their own with little or no constructive oversight or feedback along the way—or be cut from the team. At certain firms, "entrepreneurial" means doing every possible type of work from picking up someone's dry cleaning to meeting with the client's top management. And never complaining. Or bragging. Real entrepreneurs tend to do poorly in investment banking, because they're too independent and don't like working under layers of people.

 Research Tips

Good Sources of Information about Banks

Second-year MBAs who worked as summer interns in the industry

First-year associates who are alums of your school

Classmates who worked on the Street before business school

Friends of friends who work on the Street

Any alums of your school

WetFeet Insider Guides (of course!)

WetFeet.com discussion boards

Other Sources that May Also Be Helpful

Company websites

Company representatives at info sessions and career fairs

Day-on-the-job programs

Informational interviews with current employees

Business publications including the *Wall Street Journal, Investment Dealers' Digest, Institutional Investor*, and others

---

Rehearse

The second R in the lineup is rehearse. Investment banking interviews aren't a mystery. You already know what 75 percent of the interview will be: questions about you and your accomplishments. You may think this is the easy part. But most people have a hard time talking about themselves. According to our conversations with recruiters, on a schedule of ten people, several will get knocked out of the competition because they were unable to explain their accomplishments clearly and effectively and relate them to the specific job for which they are interviewing. Make sure you don't become a statistic! The best way to do this? Practice your pitch! It may sound dumb, but we recommend writing out a brief elevator pitch about who you are and what you've done. ("Elevator pitch" refers to the following scenario: Imagine that you get on an elevator with the president of the company—you now have his undivided attention for about the next 15 seconds, until he steps off the elevator. Your pitch has to be short, sweet, and convincing.) The key elements here are to convey your past accomplishments clearly, succinctly, and in a way that emphasizes the unique reason(s) why you would be the perfect candidate for the job.

The WetFeet Interview Coach

Write out your elevator pitch here. Who are you, what have you done, and why does that make you the best person for the job?

_____

_____

_____

_____

_____

_____

_____

_____

_____

_____

_____

_____

In addition to rehearsing your elevator pitch, you'll want to try to anticipate and prepare for other scenarios you are almost certain to encounter. Not only will this help you perform better, but it will help show your sensitivity to the realities of the profession. Bankers are chronically short of time, so securing a banker's undivided attention for a block of time is a privilege that should not be wasted. Come prepared. What does that mean? Here are a few suggestions from our interviewees:

- Prep yourself to discuss anything and everything that appears on your resume (and make sure you can account meaningfully for any time gaps).

- Be prepared to explain convincingly why your "greatest weakness" is actually a strength.

- Practice your handshake (firm, but not vise-like) and your ability to talk and listen while looking directly in your interviewer's eyes.

- Get comfortable with basic valuation frameworks—understanding fundamentals is more important than mastering lingo at the interview stage.

- Draft specific questions for your interviewers that will demonstrate your interest in their firm.

- Read the *Wall Street Journal* and *Business Week* to familiarize yourself with the current lay of the business land. You'll need to know at least the companies involved in any deal worth over $500 million. *Investment Dealers' Digest* is a good quarterly source for this information, and also publishes the "league tables," which rank the banks in everything from IPOs to high-yield to collateralized securities.

Because of the long hours bankers log in the office and, by correlation, with one another, candidates are often asked about the items on their resumes that might indicate whether they would make an interesting and entertaining commiserator at 2 a.m.—for example, mention of a bug collection, or a passion for pinball or paintball. Thus, you may want to include something more than the standard blue- pinstripe sort of accomplishment on your resume. The usual place to do this is in an "Other" section that should appear at the bottom of the resume. Remember, though: If you do mention your interest in medieval Japanese history, it's entirely possible that one of your interviewers will ask you what you think made the Tokugawa regime so successful—or for an even more obscure fact.

Review

Get out your old textbooks; it's time to review. Insiders tell us that investment banking interviews don't usually involve the same heavy-duty case questions found in consulting interviews. Instead, they say you're going to need to know your way around basic corporate finance and accounting issues. (If you're yawning, maybe this isn't the career for you.) Especially if you're coming from B-school. (Undergrads, breath easy: You can impress your interviewer by knowing this stuff, but it's not all de rigeur.) You should review basic concepts from CorpFin and Accounting 101. To help you with this (pop the cover, slip on the slippers, and find something to prop your eyes open), WetFeet has dusted off an old finance textbook and prepared a quick-and-dirty review of basic finance tricks that might help you in your interview.

Valuing a Company

Company valuation is perhaps the most important service provided by investment banks' corporate finance groups. Indeed, it is the heart and soul behind taking companies public, buying or selling companies, and deciding whether to repurchase stock. Accordingly, many interviewers will ask candidates (typically MBAs, though undergraduates who claim some prior valuation experience may get these questions as well) to walk through the valuation of a hypothetical enterprise. Recruiters are generally more interested in evaluating candidates' thought processes than in having candidates arrive at a particular number. However, you should at least be aware of the different methods of valuing a firm. Two of the key ones include discounted cash flow and market multiples.

Discounted Cash Flow

Theoretically, the most accurate valuation technique is the discounted cash flow (DCF) method. The assumption underlying DCF analysis is that a firm is really just a collection of projects which each throw off (or absorb) cash. Because an investor is buying the rights to these future cash flows, a firm's value is determined by valuing the net sum of these future cash flows.

Calculating DCF involves three steps: (1) estimating the future expected cash flows generated by a firm's operations; (2) choosing a discount rate which reflects the perceived uncertainty of those estimated cash flows; and (3) calculating the present value of the projected cash flows.

Determining projected future cash flows (known as pro forma cash flows) can be done several ways. An easy way is to take the current year's reported earnings (i.e., the company's after-tax net income) and multiply by some number such as the average earnings growth rate for the last five years. This gives projected net income for next year. Usually, earnings are projected for the first five to seven years, after which a terminal value is added. (The terminal value is equal to an annuity beginning in a future year, discounted back to present.) Since accounting income is often a poor proxy for cash flow, analysts will carefully calculate The Free Cash Flow by starting with EBIT (earnings before interest and taxes), taking out taxes on those earnings, and adding back interest, depreciation, amortization, and other cash-affecting items.

Although business school professors love the mathematical clarity of this means of calculating the value of a company, real bankers tell us that this method is rarely used as the key valuation technique in practice. Why? Relying on historical earnings or cash flow growth to estimate future flows is dubious, particularly in industries undergoing rapid technological change or consolidation, or experiencing heated competition. Consider the case of the deregulated telecommunications industry: Fierce competition makes firms vulnerable to a reduction in future cash flows as more companies rival for market share.

The appropriate discount rate depends on the likelihood of realizing projected cash flows. Many times, the risk-adjusted rate of return for a peer company is used, especially if the competitor's stock is already traded in the public market. While a constant discount rate is commonly used to value the stream of future cash flows, an analyst should consider whether a firm's discount rate should vary over time, reflecting different risk levels for each projected cash flow.

Taking the present value of, or discounting, future expected cash flows is relatively easy with either a handheld calculator or a spreadsheet software program (both of which will be provided by whichever bank you join). If the pro forma cash flows are the same for the time period in question, the problem reduces to the present valuation of an annuity. If the cash flows are different, then each cash flow must be discounted individually and then summed to find the present value of the cash flow bundle.

Cash Flow Formulas

Discounted Cash Flow

The basic formula for discounted cash flow analysis, at its most simple, is:

$$\frac{\text{Free Cash Flow (year 1)}}{(1 + \text{unlevered rate of return})} + \frac{\text{FCF (year 2)}}{(l + r)2} + \quad \ldots \quad + \frac{\text{FCF (year 5)}}{(l + r)5} + \text{Terminal value}$$

Free Cash flow = EBIT (earnings before interest and taxes) - estimated taxes on EBIT (at the company's

tax rate) + depreciation + amortization - capital expenditures and networking capital

requirements -/+ any other changes which will cause the company to spend cash or

be a source of cash to the company (such as severance payments or an expected

legal settlement).

Unlevered rate of return = (Risk-free rate of return + (stock beta * (return on market

portfolio - risk-free rate of return))

The risk-free rate of return is the 1-year T-Bill rate, the stock beta

comes from a standardized "beta book" produced by one of the big

investment banks or Bloomberg, and the return on a market portfolio

is the 52-week return on the S&P 500.

Terminal Value = value of an annuity in year 5 or 7 discounted back to present.

Market Multiples

While DCF is arguably the most theoretically accurate means of valuing a company, in practice, bankers rely much more heavily on the Market Multiples Method to appraise firm value. (Often DCF is used as a "reality check" on the accuracy of a multiples analysis.) Fortunately for analysts and associates, the multiples method is considerably easier and less time consuming than DCF, and is more readily understood by clients.

Multiples analysis is predicated on the assumption that markets value similarly situated firms using the same metric or set of metrics, such as a multiple of revenue, cash flow, or accounting earnings. Thus, there are essentially two steps to valuing a company using the multiples method:

1. Identify a set of comparable firms, and

2. Determine the appropriate multiples to be used.

The first step is highly subjective; it involves assessing the core business (or businesses) of the company being valued, and identifying the publicly traded companies with similar or identical core businesses. There is considerable art in appropriately defining a company's core business, even when a firm is relatively focused. Defining a firm's business determines the comparison set of companies, which in turn will determine the valuation.

The second step of multiple analysis—determining the appropriate metrics and multiples to use for valuations purposes—entails setting out the market capitalizations (that is share price multiplied by number of shares outstanding) and publicly reported financials for the various comparable firms selected in step 1, and searching for patterns in the numbers. (Typically, more-senior bankers will direct the analysts and associates working with them on where to look for patterns.) If you analyzed the pharmaceutical industry, for instance, you would find that the market capitalizations for the major players have a multiple of revenue of about 2.5 to 5x. The market capitalization of firms in other industries may be a function of different metrics: For example, department stores may trade as a multiple of total retail outlets, self-storage property operators may trade as a multiple of rental income, and so on.

Multiples analysis is an iterative process—once you complete step 2, you must step back, analyze, and evaluate whether you need to change any of the assumptions from step 1. For instance, in the pharmaceutical industry, Pfizer's market capitalization toward the end of June 2002 was about 6.5x its revenue. Obviously, if you were to include Pfizer in your average revenue multiple, you would emerge with a larger valuation for the firm you are analyzing than is probably warranted. Before discarding it, though, you must theorize why Pfizer's multiple breaks the pattern. Perhaps size justifies a higher multiple; or perhaps first-mover advantages support such a multiple. If the presumed explanation for the "outlier" multiple does not apply to the firm you are valuing, the outlying multiple should be excluded. This iterative process should continue until you have arrived at a defensible valuation, substantiated by a DCF analysis. It is mastering the art of multiples analysis that sets experienced bankers apart from their less experienced junior colleagues. Understanding at least the fundamental concept of multiples analysis at the interview stage will give you a definite advantage throughout the recruiting process.

Financial Ratios

Ratio analysis is an important part of any financial study of a firm. There are many categories of ratios, each serving a distinct purpose. It is unlikely that a candidate with no expressed familiarity with ratios would be questioned about them in an interview. Nevertheless, for the sake of thoroughness, you may want to brush up on the common financial ratios. (See box on next page.)

As with company valuation, interpreting financial ratios is more an art than a science. Generally, ratios are evaluated for a firm over time, or are compared with industry averages. Most research analysts do both. When comparing a particular ratio between periods for the same firm, you must recognize conditions that have changed between the periods being compared (different product lines or geographic markets served, changes in economic conditions, changes in prices). Similarly, when comparing ratios of a particular firm with those of similar firms, you need to see the differences (in their methods of accounting, in their operations, types of financing, etc.). Furthermore, remember that ratios based on financial statement data are necessarily subject to the same criticisms as financial statements generally—namely, that historical acquisition cost may misstate current replacement cost or net realizable value, and that firms have wide latitude in selecting from among various generally accepted accounting principles.

Key Financial Ratios

Liquidity ratios: Used to evaluate a firm's short-term liquidity, measuring its ability to pay wages, short-term creditors, taxes, and interest on bonds without delay.

Leverage ratios: Used to evaluate a firm's creditworthiness from a long-term lender's perspective.

Profitability ratios: Used by prospective or existing shareholders to evaluate a firm's past earnings, its potential for future income growth, and how much profit is paid out to shareholders in the form of dividends.

Asset-utilization ratios: Used to evaluate the productivity of firm assets.

Source: *Financial Statement Analysis: Theory, Application and Interpretation*, 6th edition, by Leopold A. Bernstein and John J. Wild (Irwin-McGraw Hill, 1997).

Even after accounting for these caveats, it is hard to say what constitutes a "healthy" ratio. General wisdom suggests an average value of 2.0 and 1.0 for the Current Ratio and Acid Test Ratio, respectively. Higher liquidity ratios are considered good, except in the case of the Cash Ratio—a very high Cash Ratio may suggest poor cash management. Leverage ratios provide a measure of how much debt a firm uses. As with most things, debt is generally considered acceptable if used in moderation. High leverage ratios indicate a firm that may be unable to repay interest and principal on time, especially during a recession, when profits tend to trend downward. However, many companies prefer to maintain higher leverage ratios because of the positive impact on asset utilization and profitability ratios.

Below are the formulas for the most widely used financial ratios.

Financial Ratio Formulas

Ratio	Formula
Liquidity Ratios	
Current	CA / CL
Acid Test (aka Quick Test)	[C + CE + MS + AR] / CL
Cash	[C + CE] / CL
Collection Period	Average AR / [CS / 360]
Days to Sell Inventory	Average I / [COR / 360]
Leverage Ratios	
Total Debt to Total Capital	[CL + LTL] / [EC + TL]
Long-Term Debt to Equity	LTL / EC
Times Interest Earned	[IBT + IE] / IE
Profitability and Investor Ratios	
Gross Profit Ratio	GP / NR
Net Income to Sales	NI / NR
Dividend Yield	DPS / MPPS
Price to Book Ratio	MPPS / BVPS
Price to Earnings Ratio	MPPS / EPS
Asset Utilization Ratios	
Sales to Fixed Assets	NR / Average FA
Sales to Total Assets	NR / Average TA
Sales to Inventories	NR / Average I

Table of Abbreviations

Abbreviations	Account Name	Financial Statement
AR	Accounts Receivable	Balance Sheet
BVPS	Book Value Per Share	Balance Sheet
C	Cash	Balance Sheet
CA	Current Assets	Balance Sheet
CE	Cash Equivalents	Balance Sheet
CL	Current Liabilities	Balance Sheet
COR	Cost of Revenue	Income Statement
CS	Credit Sales	Income Statement
DPS	Dividends Per Share	None
EC	Equity Capital	Balance Sheet
EPS	Earnings Per Share	Income Statement
FA	Fixed Assets	Balance Sheet
GP	Gross Profit	Income Statement
I	Inventory	Balance Sheet
IBT	Income Before Taxes	Income Statement
IE	Interest Expense	Income Statement
LTL	Long-Term Liabilities	Balance Sheet
MPPS	Market Price Per Share	None
MS	Marketable Securities	Balance Sheet
NI	Net Income	Income Statement
NR	Net Revenues	Income Statement
TA	Total Assets	Balance Sheet
TL	Total Liabilities	Balance Sheet
TO	Turnover	None

Note: Per share values come from financial statement values, which are divided by the number of common shares outstanding.

Financing Strategies for Companies

If you're applying for an investment banking job, your interviewers will assume that you have a solid understanding of the financial aspects of managing a company. Just in case you don't, here's the basic info. Generally speaking, companies obtain the funds they need to sustain growth by selling stock (equity) or borrowing (debt); by retaining earnings (not distributing profits to shareholders); and/or by selling off (divesting) noncore, nonstrategic assets. The corporate finance group of an investment bank advises companies on how to most efficiently and cost-effectively finance growth. Corporate finance works with salespeople, traders, and research analysts to determine the best ways a company might do this.

Staying Abreast of Current Events

Being knowledgeable of current events, financial and otherwise, is imperative, both during the interview process and beyond. Expect an interviewer to ask you about current events, especially financial activities in the U.S. or abroad. The *Wall Street Journal* is widely read (why do you think it gets away with having "Wall Street" in its title?). Publications with a more international flavor include the *Financial Times* and the *Economist*.

The *Wall Street Journal* (*WSJ*) has three principal sections. (A fourth section detailing arts and leisure activities is now included in the Friday issue, but as an I-banker, you won't need that.) The first section provides the reader with general economic, political, and business news. Reading the first-page mini-summaries of news happenings takes little time and provides an excellent overview of what's going on in the world. Section B includes articles about management, law, marketing, and technology. A wide variety of financial tables are included in Section C. If you are a student, you should call the educational division of Dow Jones, Inc., to get a summary of how to understand the financial tables.

An investment banker must know how to read stock tables too—after all, that's where the money is made. One of the most important, the New York Stock Exchange Composite Transactions, provides information on stocks listed on the New York Stock Exchange. Information is also provided for stocks traded on the American Stock Exchange and in the over-the-counter market via the NASDAQ (National Association of Securities Dealers Automatic Quotations) system. While explanatory notes for some tables are provided in each issue of the *Wall Street Journal*, it is worthwhile illustrating how information is reported. Check out the following page for an explanation of a listing for the General Electric Corporation.

General Electric's Stock Listing

52 Weeks Hi	52 Weeks Lo	Stock	Sym	Div	Yld %	PE	Vol 100s	Hi	Lo	Close	Net Chg
$96^7/_8$	59	GenElec	GE	1.20	1.5	31	96588	$82^1/_4$	$78^3/_8$	$81^7/_8$	+6

The columns on the left reveal that the stock traded in a range from $59 to $96.875 over the last 52 weeks. This price range has been adjusted for various types of distributions to share-holders, such as stock splits and share dividends. (And if you bought it at $59 and sold at its high, you'd have made $37.87 a share, less 30 percent capital gains. Not bad.)

The next column provides an abbreviated company name, followed by the ticker symbol of the stock.

"Div" is a measure of the dividend per share paid to shareholders. In this case, shareholders were paid a healthy $1.20 per share.

The dividend yield of 1.5 is a measure of the dollar dividend relative to the price per share of the stock. A stock price of $80 would yield 1.5 percent from the dividend of $1.20.

The PE, or price-earnings ratio, says that the price per share ($80) is about 31 times earnings per share. PE multiples vary over time and business cycles.

Multiply the volume number by 100 to obtain an estimate of the number of shares traded of this stock on the previous trading day.

The stock traded on the previous day within a range of $78.375 and $82.25, and closed at $81.875 per share, six dollars higher than the prior day's close.

Excerpted from the *Wall Street Journal*, 09/09/98.

The Interview

General Accounting Information

A public company must publicly disclose audited financial information at the close of each quarter, and must report a full 12 months of financial results at the end of their fiscal year every year. Many companies file their 12-month reports on a calendar year basis while other firms elect a twelve-month period corresponding to their natural production cycles. There are four primary financial statements: balance sheet, income statement, statement of cash flows, and statement of retained earnings.

The balance sheet. The balance sheet is a snapshot of a firm's assets, liabilities, and equity on the reporting date. Assets typically include current or short-term assets like cash, accounts receivable, and inventory; fixed assets such as depreciable equipment; and intangible assets like patents and trademarks. Liabilities include current obligations such as accounts payable and long-term debt. Shareholders' equity consists of all the various types of stock outstanding plus accumulated retained earnings. Relying exclusively on the balance sheet may be misleading: At times, firms engage in "window dressing" (actions taken to strengthen the balance sheet for the particular reporting date). In addition, because assets are recorded at their historical values (their market values at the time they were first acquired), when the market value of assets declines, historical value overestimates the strength of the firm. Balance sheets may underestimate the financial health of a firm as well. For example, assets such as a talented, productive labor force are not recorded. Yet, superior firms are often market leaders in large part because of their talented employees and managers.

Income statement (aka profit and loss statement). The income statement records information about revenue, expenses, and profit for the firm—how much money the firm made or lost in a given period. Although this is the basic statement used to determine whether a company is profitable or not, bankers will take a careful look at the numbers here to understand what they really mean. To the extent that financial accounting standards allow firm managers to record income statement items using one of several different alternatives, the quality of earnings—also known as the bottom line—varies over time and across companies. Often a financial analyst will make adjustments to reflect the extent to which a particular financial accounting policy choice renders accounting income higher or lower than actual cash income. For example, if a firm's depreciable assets are vulnerable to technological obsolescence and the firm uses a very long depreciation period, recorded expenses will underestimate depreciation costs. Reported income will therefore be overstated accordingly.

Cash flow statement. The statement of cash flows is another essential part of any financial analysis. After all, even though a company may be profitable, it needs cash to pay its bills and fund its ongoing operations. Think of your own personal finances. If your tuition bill is due, but you just opened your bank account and they tell you that you can't write checks for another 30 days, you could be in trouble—even though you have more than enough resources to cover your expenses. Companies won't normally have trouble with bank waiting periods, but they will often be balancing their outflows (paying bills, employees, and so on) with their inflows (cash from sales of products, collections of amounts owed to the company, and investment). The cash flow report explains how cash was used and generated in each of three areas: operating, financing, and investing. Operating cash flows are those funds consumed and generated by the operation of the company's core business. For example, the production, distribution, and sale of widgets. Financing cash flows describe events such as the payment of dividends, the issuance of stock or bonds, stock repurchases, and the repayment of debt. Investing cash flows detail how money was spent or raised from selling or buying capital.

Statement of retained earnings. The statement of retained earnings is used mostly for analyzing the relationship between dividends and retained earnings. It shows how end-of-year retained earnings are computed. To calculate, start with beginning-of-year retained earnings, add net income, and subtract dividends paid.

typical financial analysis relies on all four reports. Footnotes to the statements .re found in the back of the annual report and must be used to understand how financial information should best be interpreted.

Stock Analysis

Stock analysis is an integral component of a research analyst's responsibilities, and is relevant to the sales and trading functions as well. Moreover, interviewers will often ask you to discuss a particular stock or stocks you follow, and give a "buy" or "sell" recommendation. In such cases, the interviewer is looking more to establish your interest in the financial markets than to debate the merits of a particular company or its stock price. A good answer to a question such as "Tell me about a stock that you follow" would be to give a brief background about the company and industry and why it interests you. You should then follow with a brief discussion of the current stock price, how it has changed over time, what seems to be driving the price up or down, and the relevant industry information.

Among stock pickers, this type of analysis is known as fundamental analysis (the other main type of analysis is known as technical analysis—or "charting"—and focuses on the historical pattern of prices and volume with the objective of discerning patterns in supply and demand over a specified period of time). When a pro does it (that would be you, once you get a banking job), fundamental analysis begins with the underlying factors that drive a particular industry and firms within that industry. While historical information is used, pro forma or forecasted information is also employed. Thus, fundamental analysis starts with a "big picture" evaluation of the economy and proceeds to narrow its scope to a study of industry-level metastructure. A detailed analysis of each company operating within a particular industry follows, culminating in the creation of a predictive valuation model. This company-level analysis entails both an assessment of a firm's financial profile as well as "softer" issues such as management competency, strategic vision, and brand equity.

Several comments are in order with respect to fundamental analysis. First, it is meaningless to analyze a firm in isolation. Most bankers either analyze a firm over time or against an industry benchmark or both. Moreover, you should only begin analyzing financial statements after you've examined the fundamentals of the industry. For example, if you were a research analyst covering the pharmaceutical industry, you might identify overseas sales as a key industry driver. In analyzing a particular pharmaceutical company's income statement, you'd know to account for the fact that exchange rate fluctuations will affect period-to-period earnings considerably.

Comparing Two Firms

Calculating and benchmarking individual ratios is a necessary, but insufficient, part of the study of a firm's financial health. It is also necessary to decompose (or "double-click on") the ratios, or employ several ratios to describe a firm's financial well-being. Consider abbreviated financial information for two firms, ABC and XYZ, both operating in the same industry.

6/26/02 9:37 a.m.

	Firm ABC	Firm XYZ
Price Per Unit	$10	$5
Number of Units Sold	1,000,000	2,000,000
Sales Revenue	$10,000,000	$10,000,000
Cost of Goods Sold	$8,000,000	$6,000,000
Net Income	$2,000,000	$4,000,000
Net Profit Margin	20%	40%

At first blush, Firms ABC and XYZ seem to be equally successful, each generating $10 million in sales revenue. However, further inspecting the numbers reveals two significant facts. First, Firm XYZ sells twice as many units as Firm ABC and at a lower price. Second, ABC's expenses are 33 percent higher than XYZ's, pushing its net profit margin downward. To derive a robust predictive model that can be used to value a firm and its stock, an analyst must understand the operating profiles of the various competitors within an industry.

Investment Banker-Speak

Part of your research should involve learning to "talk the talk." You're not expected to have mastered banker-speak by the time you have your first interview, but you can separate yourself from a very large pack if you become familiar with some job-related terms. (Note: The source for some of these buzzwords is Miriam Naficy's *Fast Track*, full of other useful tips.)

Banker/I-banker. As with most professions, investment banking has its own patois. While you will find, sprinkled throughout this guide, many of the buzzwords you should become comfortable with, one bit of lingo is worth highlighting at the outset: Calling investment bankers "I-bankers" is like calling San Francisco "San Fran" or "'Frisco"—only the out-of-towners do it, and the locals will immediately know you're not one of their own. Get into the habit of using the term "banker."

Beauty contest. The series of presentations investment banks make to clients to make themselves more appealing than competitors and therefore win the deal. Think of your efforts to land a position in investment banking as your own personal beauty contest.

Bond. A form of tradable debt evidenced by a promise to pay back money owed. The issuer of a bond promises to pay the bondholder a specific amount of interest (aka the coupon) on the original amount borrowed (aka the principal) for a specified length of time.

Cash flow. The amount of real dollars a company generates from its operating, investing, and financing activities. In many industries, cash flow differs from reported income (profit) because of noncash accounting charges that must be included in reported income. Therefore, cash flow is often a better measure of a firm's health. Cash flow is often equated with EBITDA ("ee-bit-dah")—earnings before interest, taxes, depreciation, and amortization.

Copy, collate, spiral binding, double-sided . . . Enough said.

Comparables/Compsave. Large spreadsheets comparing the financial stats of different deals, client competitors, or even the investment banking capabilities of competing firms. As an analyst, you will spend a significant portion of your waking hours updating these and ensuring their accuracy (and dreaming about them in your sleeping hours); as an associate, you will oversee their preparation and double-check for accuracy.

Corporate finance. The group within an investment bank that provides advice to corporations on a range of financial matters, including raising capital via debt or equity.

Due diligence, or due dili (Di´-lee). Investment bankers' evaluation of the financial and other conditions of a company before they help the company issue securities to the public.

Equity or stock. An ownership interest in a company, publicly or privately held.

Fixed income. Also known as bonds. As the name indicates, the interest rate is fixed, with a certain period of maturity.

IPO. Initial public offering: Selling shares of a privately held company to the public for the first time.

Junk bonds (high-yield debt). Bonds backed by issuers with shaky financial prospects. To compensate for the increased risk of default (i.e., the possibility that the issuer will be unable to make scheduled interest or principal repayments), the interest rate demanded on junk debt is relatively high.

LBO. Leveraged buy out. Buying a company using predominantly borrowed funds, often through a combination of debt securities and bank loans. For a number of reasons, including bad press in the late 1980s and subsequent changes in bank lending regulations, LBOs are now often referred to as HLTs (highly leveraged transactions).

Model. Comprehensive financial projections, created with Lotus or Excel spreadsheets, that show the effect of a specific transaction. Check one out. You will spend a great deal of your time building, updating, and explaining these.

Pitch books. The documents investment banks use to try to win business with potential clients at beauty contests. The book highlights the bank's performance, merits, and, of course, the comps and models you slaved over. This is what you stay up until all hours compiling, editing, and, yes, copying, collating, and binding.

Spell check. Swear by it from here on out. Two minutes before the big meeting is the wrong moment to catch a typo. (You'll also need a new pair of reading glasses and a dictionary always within easy reach.)

Underwriting. Investment banks' purchase of a securities issue for resale to investors.

Yield. The annual return on an investment, expressed as a percentage of the original investment.

Interview Prep Guide

- The Judge's Scorecard
- Acing the Interview
- Body Language Dos and Don'ts
- Round 1: First Interview
- The Airplane Test
- Round 2 and Beyond
- Social Gatherings . . . From Cocktails to Lunch
- Your Final Interview
- A Few Words on the Stress Interview
- Your Turn to Ask the Questions
- Denouement
- The Offer
- Dealing With the Offer
- Salary Negotiations

The Judge's Scorecard

As we noted at the outset, the skills, personality, and day-to-day demands vary greatly among the various areas of investment banking. In this section, we'll tell you what the recruiters in CorpFin and Sales & Trading are seeking. Not surprisingly, recruiters for each area look for different qualities in candidates. Contrary to popular opinion, however, quantitative abilities and a degree in finance will only get you so far, regardless of the area for which you are interviewing. Recruiters and, more importantly, VPs and managing directors tell us that they are looking for that much less easily defined "right personality" and "fire in your belly." Insiders admit that a candidate's enthusiasm, ability to interact well with others, and respect for the serious responsibilities investment banking jobs entail are just as important as raw intelligence. It's surprisingly easy to forget in all this that vast sums of money will be entrusted, however briefly, to your care. Moreover, it's never your money. Act as if it were and you'll win important points.

 Investment Banking Recruiters' Top Ten Pet Peeves

1. Being asked personal questions (especially regarding even the most obvious pregnancy).
2. Candidates who read their resumes during the interview. (Don't you know your own background?)
3. Follow-up calls to confirm that the firm received your resume.
   (Recruiters sometimes get 8,000 resumes a season.)
4. E-mailed resumes.
5. "Creative" resumes (strange paper and fonts, attached to a fishing reel hook).
6. Questions that have already been covered in the interview.
7. Canned answers.
8. Long-winded answers.
9. Arrogance.
10. An undergrad who thinks he or she is going to be running meetings and rubbing elbows with the CEO.

Corporate Finance

You sincerely want to sell yourself as an ideal CorpFin candidate, but you're still a bit unclear what specifically recruiters want the ideal hire to be. Okay, here it is: They're looking for strong quantitative and analytical skills (good with numbers, able to draw conclusions from seemingly unrelated facts); an understanding of the industry (quick—what was the biggest IPO last year?); an ability to learn quickly and work efficiently (never need things explained twice, never miss deadlines); a meticulous attention to detail (it's done right, done fast, and done perfectly—the first time); and an ability to juggle multiple complex assignments simultaneously (can manage three Type A personalities who all expect their projects completed yesterday).

Special Information for Undergraduates

Recruiters sum up their ideal analyst candidate for corporate finance as an economics, finance, or business major who has graduated from one of the top 40 schools with a minimum 3.5 GPA. The candidate has demonstrated excellence through academic awards and the ability to juggle a rigorous schedule of extracurricular leadership activities and training for a team sport. Oh yes, lest we forget, Mr. or Ms. Ideal Candidate also boasts stellar SAT scores and fluency in Spanish and Mandarin.

Of course, recruiters can dream just like the rest of us. In reality, there are actually very few candidates that fit this idealized profile—so take heart! In fact, whether you realize it or not, you too share many of the qualities of the ideal candidate, even if your experiences and talents aren't quite as instantly marketable as those listed above. While you may not have an athletic bone in your body or an economics degree, you are committed to something. Highlight it! So much the better if it's related to finance. Insiders say that though their banks tend to favor people from quantitative disciplines, liberal arts majors are not banned from the pool (note: that's about as encouraging a statement as an investment banking recruiter is likely to utter, so don't feel discouraged). However, you'll want to do whatever you can to persuade your interviewers that you possess the necessary analytical and quantitative skills. At least one accounting or economics course and a fairly sophisticated understanding of the industry are also necessary. Be prepared to demonstrate that your supreme powers of analysis were honed through X, Y, and Z experiences. At the end of the day, most liberal arts majors who get hired have been interns in some area of finance and know the markets. Nevertheless, according to one source, one of his firm's better choices in a recent year was a history major with excellent research and writing skills.

It's also important to remember that getting hired as an undergraduate analyst is based more on intangibles than any other position in the bank. One firm actually tried recently to find a correlation between its most successful hires and the schools they went to, their grades, their SAT scores, their "rating" on Super Saturday, and other quantifiable items on a candidate's resume. They found none. Use this to your advantage. Those of you who can demonstrate an understanding and real enthusiasm for the job, attention to detail, and a friendly disposition and a humble eagerness to follow directions may be way ahead of your peers who took accounting for four years straight.

Recruiters know that an undergraduate's experience is limited, so make them see that you are, in the words of one insider, "reachable, teachable, and updateable," not to mention full of determination and easy to get along with. If you can demonstrate that you can survive, thrive, and take orders in a Type A environment, much of the objective "ideal candidate" criteria above may magically disappear. Don't forget humility. No one likes an overconfident 22-year-old (or, worse, 21-year-old) know-it-all. One recruiter recalls an interview with a recent hire who possessed the perfect combination of modesty and understatement. "Everyone recommended this guy. While he attended a school where we don't recruit, no one seemed to care. This guy was just so nice and so into the job that everyone unanimously agreed he would sell his soul to get his work done. His intelligence, ambition, and humility made him an ideal analyst."

Insider Tip

Be prepared to demonstrate that your supreme powers of analysis were honed through X, Y, and Z experiences.

Special Information for MBAs

While an increasing percentage of the full-time associate classes are hired from the summer associate pool, there is still hope for those of you who elected a different demanding (or not so demanding) first-year summer—provided, of course, you've done time in banking or have relevant work experience in areas in which the firm specializes. The necessary criteria for an associate include all the expectations investment banks have for undergraduates and summer associates, plus total grasp of the business and the job. While your undergraduate studies, GPA, GMATs, and SATs matter, your work experience, the reputation of the business school you attended, and your potential to become a long-term asset to the firm are far more important. Of course, raw brainpower is a must, since they're expecting that you can easily learn anything your background left out.

When asked what she looks for in an ideal associate candidate, one recruiter says: "We don't look for one certain thing. We look for a good record of achievement in undergraduate grades, extracurricular, and post-college work experience. We pay special attention if they were promoted early, worked in a Big [Five] firm, ranked in the top tier of an analyst class, or served in the armed forces. Undergraduate majors are not as important at this stage. Of course, my ideal candidate would have a finance and accounting degree and have worked as an analyst at another firm. I love that because then we don't have to train them."

She notes that as a result, "It's not surprising that 30 percent of the investment banking class were former analysts."

Another recruiter says, "My ideal candidate would be at a top business school and would have been an analyst at Goldman or Morgan. He or she would have language skills, which are now more important than ever. They would also have done something different for their MBA summer and bring something new to the table."

Sales and Trading

The hard and soft criteria used to assess people for sales and trading jobs are a bit different from those in corporate finance. Sales and trading interviews are more heavily skewed toward assessing people skills, particularly those related to negotiation, relationship-building, and persuasion. If you're not sure why, take a stroll around a trading floor when it's busy and then, when you've had enough, go find the library or corporate finance department. Clock how long it takes before you really want off the trading floor, and pay attention to how you feel re-entering a sane and calm milieu. If the answers are "almost instantly" and "much better," you're going for the wrong job. Those of you who just could not bear to tear yourselves away, think you're plenty tough enough to swim with even the most egotistical sharks, and would have no problem risking several million dollars every few minutes for seven and a half hours a day are probably ready for at least a trial. A brand-name school and high GPA mean next to nothing once you're working on a sales or trading floor. Rather, "What have you done lately?" becomes the yardstick for success, and your people skills will largely determine your ability to measure up.

The various desks grudgingly willing to hire young talent are looking for market smarts. (Lest you forget, while you're learning, you're not earning. Playing teacher to a crop of fresh recruits is a much more direct hit on the desk's bottom line than anywhere in CorpFin.) Intelligence is measured by your understanding of the markets and specific products, as well as your quantitative skills and ability to take orders faster than the fastest online system. While investment bankers frequently schmooze with clients over long lunches, traders would never consider interrupting their work for daytime social engagements. In fact, for many months, your title will be vice president in charge of take-out. And if you want to survive, you'll haul in those

 On Analysts

As one insider chillingly puts it, "Analysts are not bankers, they are slaves to the bankers. We want to see that they'll do as they are told." According to this same source, you won't be making corporate presentations to senior management, but you will become best friends with the copier and spend many a night sleeping on it.

hamburgers and pizzas and groaning tubs of guacamole with all the good cheer you can muster. From the get-go, you must rev yourself up into overdrive and start talking, moving, listening, and networking faster than you ever thought imaginable. The good news? Next year, you'll be trading and selling with the pros—and mercilessly "managing" the new kids.

Special Information for Undergraduates

Students with high GPAs who have majored in economics or finance generally fill undergraduate sales and trading positions. Understanding economics is a prerequisite to surviving the first three months. One source reveals that she generally looks for resumes that show a willingness to take risks, sales experience, and nontraditional choices. Since most college graduates know very little about the markets at the outset, your personality is what really counts. If you come across as a confident (but not cocky), thick-skinned, good-natured person who learns quickly and can work on a team, you're a strong candidate. Liberal arts majors are rarely hired unless they have prior S&T intern experience.

Special Information for MBAs

Sales and trading candidates have to pass a different muster from whatever their pals are undergoing over in CorpFin. S&T recruiters want to be convinced that your past experiences and unwavering passion for the markets make you the logical choice for the job. They also typically require that second-year MBAs have previous experience on the Street. Asked to describe what she looks for in an ideal candidate, a bulge-bracket recruiter says, "The person would have graduated from a top-tier undergraduate and graduate program, having demonstrated excellence both academically and in some activity that required them to be a team player. Previous Wall Street experience of course is ideal; however, consulting experience is also great. Quantitative skills are a must for anyone in any of the sales and trading positions." She adds, a bit regretfully, that "as of late we've been tightening up on our hiring practices, but we're accustomed to taking people from a wide range of backgrounds. We hire people ranging from commercial bankers to pharmaceutical salesmen to former attorneys. The candidate must be a self-starter and have proven they can take an ambiguous situation and successfully make it work."

The S&T interviewing process has fewer instant and obvious faux pas. Where you went to school is generally much less important than a profound, if not intuitive, understanding of the business. The bottom line is money. Indeed, if you're asked, "Why do you want to be a trader?" and you answer, "I want to give it my all and make a ton of money," chances are your interviewer would just shrug and move on to the next question. (Over in investment-banking land, of course, such a response would likely summon forth a large hook from behind the curtains that would yank you offstage.) If you're a potentially quick moneymaker and you seem tough enough to survive, then you're in—at least for a while, until you do something unpardonably stupid or you just cost too much, and then you're out. Cocky arrogance is one of the instant faux pas.

Insiders confess they hate when the new MBAs start interviewing on the floor. One says with a sigh, "You can just tell that they think they are going to walk in and start trading. Little do they know that they'll be responsible for getting coffee for someone younger and less educated—and that generally doesn't fly too well." Titles mean very little in S&T unless you are really senior. Basically, you're either a peon or a moneymaker. One recruiter adds, "Past successes mean very little to us. . . . You must be inwardly focused and driven, but if you can't thrive in an aggressive team atmosphere, you're history. That's why we hire so many athletes."

A final tip: When you interview on the floor, make sure you have a clear understanding of what you want to do there. If you want to work with derivatives, have a reason and know the product. Don't ever pretend you know more than you actually do. Traders and salespeople revel in foolish displays of ignorance. You haven't experienced humiliation, complete and utter ignominy, until a trader decides to dress you down in public for saying something really dumb.

 Favorite Interview Gaffes

Heavy cologne

Poor eye contact

Casual language (greeting an interviewer with "Hey, what's up?")

Sloppy appearance

Cold or clammy hands

Answering a different question from the one you were asked

Nervous chatter—don't be afraid of a brief moment of silence

True confessions (keep your political, social, love, and any other personal topics to yourself, and whatever you do, don't ask your interviewer about his or hers!)

Summer Internships

Banks require the same levels of commitment and enthusiasm from their summer hires as from their full-time recruits. Recruiters maintain, "We don't expect first-year MBAs to know everything." However, a recent MBA hire debunks this: "Even though recruiters tell you as an intern they don't expect you to know what it is that you want to do, they are lying. It's a competitive pool out there, so you'd better express if you are interested in equity versus fixed income and why you are suited to the job." What the people in charge of hiring really mean, then, is that summer interns can't possibly know what all of those analysts who slaved over copy machines at 4 a.m. for two to three years before business school know. You bring "other advantages" to the firm—it's up to you to figure out what those advantages might be and how to sell them to the summer program you want most.

Here's what recruiters say they look for when interviewing summer interns:

- Excellence in some field—be it athletics, the military, short-story writing, professional music engagements

- Dedication—which can be translated into a passion for proofreading pitch books

- A good, steady track record—not just one brilliant success, but consistent diligence and competence

- Type A personality (if you're not sure what this means, you probably don't have one)

- Good business sense—even without experience, the instincts should be there

- Good grades in B-school (Your undergraduate grades don't matter too much unless you got Ds in finance or accounting. Admission to a top business school will have bleached the writing on the slate.)

Special Information for Undergraduates

Many fewer firms offer pregraduation summer analyst programs for undergraduates (though a handful, most notably CSFB, have longstanding, formal programs). Consequently, recruiters are much less concerned about Wall Street–specific experience when interviewing analyst candidates than associate hopefuls. At the same time, of course, having a summer analyst program under your belt enhances your marketability immeasurably by distinguishing you with a seal of approval from the Street.

Special Information for MBAs

It used to be easy and acceptable for MBA students to explore one career option in the summer after their first year, and then, upon graduation, take a job in a completely different field. Insiders caution that investment banking firms are now putting more and more stock in the summer internship—if you want to try something totally different and then move to Wall Street upon graduation, you may have trouble. Many companies find it easier and less expensive to fill their associate class with former summer interns than to expand the second-year campus recruiting and interviewing effort. This has resulted in a much more demanding screening process for MBAs. But keep in mind that MBA recruiters don't require previous Wall Street experience from first-years seeking summer associate positions.

Research

Junior research positions involve a great deal of modeling. (Remember models? Lotus and Excel spreadsheets with zillions of little numbers all over them?) These slots are rarely filled by liberal arts majors unless they've studied a lot of accounting. Even then, your life's work to date would likely have to have included total immersion in an industry of importance to an investment bank—such as software or surface transportation—plus a rigorous stint on a Dow Jones rewrite desk. You need excellent writing skills, well-honed editing abilities, and the ability to sell via numbers the companies your firm is underwriting.

Acing the Interview

Now that you have a handle on the various departments in the bank, you've done your three Rs (remember, that's Research, Rehearse, and Review), and you have a handle on what the recruiters will be seeking, it's time for that mad dash through the interview process. If you're serious about entering this field, chances are good that you'll have a series of back-to-back interviews with many of the firms in the industry. In this section, we'll tell you how the process will unfold, and provide recommendations on how to succeed at each stage of the interview process. We start with a few general tips to help you throughout the process.

Picking Your Time

Can you position yourself to stay in the recruiters' minds based on the time of day you meet with them? Psychological studies have explored in some depth when and how to catch your interviewer's most positive biorhythms. Most of this research says that the first interview is traditionally forgotten, the last is barely visible through the blur of exhaustion, and those poor souls interviewed just after lunch are either turned into the end of a turkey sandwich or a nap. Insiders reveal that they do indeed tend to forget the first candidate, unless of course he or she is a superstar, in which case it's a very good slot—the interviewer's mind is made up and everyone else gets short shrift. When all is said and done, the bottom line is: If you have a choice, sign up for a time when you are typically most awake and coherent. Your own energy can often be the most contagious and important aspect of the meeting.

What to Wear

If you don't have one already, go out and buy yourself an interview suit. One that fits properly and looks sober (sober, not somber). Gentlemen, leave the suspenders at home. Don't forget to shine your shoes and shave. Ladies, your favorite pantsuit is not an option; your choice is skirts or dresses only. In addition, please keep in mind the "dollar rule," which requires that hemlines be no higher than the width of a dollar bill above your knees. If it's a straight, narrow skirt, extend this rule to sitting down. Sound unbearably dowdy? Get past it. Think instead what your bonus next year will buy. For reasons that probably have more to do with control than we want to explore right now, recruiters actually like the idea that investment banking is one of the last bastions of conformity. It's all about fitting into a culture. As one interviewer puts it, "We don't want anyone who's too creative; we want everyone to dress the same to keep up our image. It's better to blend in than stand out." He remembers with a shudder one candidate who "pranced into my office unshaven. My thought was that if he doesn't have time or the respect to shave, he's not interested. Remember, getting hired is tough. We are looking for ways to cut people. If it comes down to two people with the same credentials and personality, the one dressed like a banker will inevitably get the job."

Readers, when dressing for your interview try to follow one simple rule: Never look better than the bride. Save those unstructured Armani suits and outrageous ties for the night you celebrate your offer. It is guaranteed they won't be appreciated in your interview. Outfit yourself in quiet gray or navy, and carry a leather-bound notebook complete with pen slot (and pen), a short writing sample, and, of course, several extra copies of your resume.

Thank-You Notes

The jury is still out regarding thank-you notes. Recruiters say that thank-you notes usually do more harm than good, since more often than not there's at least one typo. (Remember: Typos are a sure-fire way to undo any success you've had at convincing recruiters of your thoroughness and attention to detail.) However, the consensus seems to be that bankers and the people on the trading floor love them (thank-you notes, not typos). We have even heard of several instances where a thank-you note inspired a salesperson or trader to call the recruiter on behalf of the candidate. About the only concession recruiters were willing to make was that thank-you notes after the final round are a good indicator as to whether or not you are going to accept an offer. One recruiter reports, "I definitely look at them. But they generally don't change my opinion of a candidate either way. However, it is important to various bankers you interview with. It can alter their opinion." Another source acknowledges that she nearly reconsidered a candidate who sent an excellent thank-you note after he was rejected. But the keyword here is "nearly," and in banking "nearly" is never enough. (Check out the WetFeet Insider Guide Effective Job Search Communication for more information on crafting effective thank-you notes.)

Body Language Dos and Don'ts

Do

- Greet with a smile and a firm handshake.

- Sit down only after your interviewer does.

- Sit up straight and look alert.

- Make steady eye contact with your interviewer, especially when you're listening.

- Lean forward when answering a difficult question (it signals that you're interested and not intimidated).

- Smile every so often. Not too much and never forced. One genuine smile is always worth waiting for.

- Exude calm. Keep your voice low and your hands in your lap.

- Wear clothes and shoes that fit you properly.

Don't

- Stare your interviewer down.

- Lean back in a chair or cross your legs.

- Fidget with pens or any other stray accessories you might have in your possession.

- Make dramatic hand gestures to reinforce your point.

- Smile the whole time. It may be interpreted as nervousness or, worse yet, emptiness.

- Slouch.

- Take off your shoes, jacket, or any other piece of clothing.

- Interrupt or look like you want to interrupt.

- Look at your watch.

- Bite your nails, touch your face, fix your hair.

Round 1: First Interview

Welcome to the career center or, if you're lucky, a stale hotel room. You have an appointment for 10:30 a.m. and Mr. or Ms. 10:00 is taking up your precious time. No need to raise your anxiety level any higher than it is already; your time will come soon enough. The interviewer, who may be from human resources, a junior associate, or a mid-level banker, ushers out your predecessor, shuts the door to make some quick notes, and then invites you in. This is the bell for round one. Whether you find yourself facing one or two interviewers, it's time to turn it on. Questions are usually straightforward, veering into the technical if you appear to know something about the job already. The recruiter, who is more often than not an alumnus, will try to get a sense of your background, what you're like as a person, and how capable you are. As one recruiter puts it, "Once we assess that they have the raw brain power, we're happy. We can easily train them."

The interview is your chance to focus on your achievements rather than that low GMAT score or the second-semester C in accounting (although you may well be asked to explain these). It's also your chance to tell them what they want to hear. Presumably you followed our advice and paid careful attention to what they said they care about most in that initial campus information session. We don't advise you to parrot their exact words, but a judiciously paraphrased regurgitation will serve you well. If Bank X asserted back in September that teamwork and doing right by the customer matter more than net income and *Institutional Investor* research ratings combined, these are what matter to you, too. You can even point to several seemingly irrelevant items on your resume which, with a bit of earnest explanation, demonstrate your dedication to team and ethics. (Not totally irrelevant items, mind you, and the earnest explanation had better be well rehearsed and credible.)

Mr. or Ms. Interviewer will probably begin th5vey to them that you know the difference between a managing director (feudal lord) and an analyst (humble serf)—though the more substantive questions pertaining to your role won't emerge until later rounds.

A Few Words on Humility

Don't be shy about touting your accomplishments on your resume or in your interviews. An excess of modesty won't get you the job. For example, as an associate, you will likely be responsible for managing a team of analysts as well as maintaining client relationships. If you've had any relevant managerial experience at all (babysitting three kids for ten days while their parents were on vacation qualifies), don't hold back. At the same time, if you have been taking credit for everything you have ever lent a hand to, give it up now. Demonstrate that you are committed to that future and know when and how to metamorphose, gracefully, from team player into leader. Regardless of how much time you agonized over the sand castle after everyone else went swimming, you must be eager and willing to present the finished product as a group effort. Equally important, restraining your humility does not mean denying your fallibility. Indeed, addressing a mistake and discussing what you learned and how you grew as a result of the experience demonstrates maturity and self-confidence—two traits investment banks seek in new recruits.

Special Information for Undergraduates

Package and present your responses as though you're interviewing for a job as the firm's English butler. If you can convince your interviewers that all you want in life is to work 80 hours a week, do what you are told and do it perfectly, be a part of their firm, and learn a lot, then you're well on your way to an offer. Your job in this process is easier than that of the MBA hopefuls in that you really only have to convince these folks that you are readily trainable and would be enjoyable to work with for the next two to three years. They're looking for smart, diligent workers, not the next CFO.

As an analyst hopeful, you'll probably also be asked how you arrived at the decision to pursue investment banking. Have a thoughtful response prepared and make sure your interviewer understands: It's not just investment banking, it's this firm that's the compelling draw. One recruiter always asks candidates to explain an important choice they made and how it affected them. In her considerable experience, "A true sign of maturity is an ability to analyze yourself and the decisions you have made." Previous work experience is important, and a job that required fairly rigorous time management tells your interviewers you have the stamina and ability to successfully juggle your responsibilities. Focus on the skills involved, not the prestige of the job—it's not the job that matters; it's what you learned from it. Short-order cooks, for example, know how to handle stress and make a seemingly endless stream of either/or decisions. Thus, you can and should discuss these skills in the abstract. Also, if you worked your way through college, be sure to highlight it.

In addition, talk about your experiences on a sports team or in a group to which you dedicated a great deal of time. The school newspaper, chorus, and debating society are all just as valid "team" credits, but you're going to have to work a little harder to explain why. Merely listing your accomplishments doesn't work here. You have to use them to illustrate what a willing and capable person you are, your countless interests, and your drive to succeed in anything to which you put your young mind. Whip out a few examples that show you're quantitatively savvy (especially if you are a liberal arts major) as well as qualitatively aware (especially if you never wrote a seriously analytical paper your four years in college). And never forget that your body language in this round is speaking louder than your words. If you say you're really interested in the job and that you understand stressful time management better than most of your classmates, make sure your nonverbal cues support these statements.

Recruiter's FAQ. When we asked recruiters to list some other frequently asked questions, the list looked something like this:

- What makes a good salesperson?

- What makes a good product?

- Pitch me a stock.

- Ask me a good trading question.

- Why are you interested in sales and trading?

- Explain your role in the such-and-such job listed on your resume.

- Tell me about your biggest failure. [One recruiter admits if a person can't talk about failure, or if he or she puts too quick and rosy a spin on a very small shortcoming, that's a red flag. In this business, you can't let your ego get in the way and you have to be able to admit when you have screwed up.]

- How would you feel about selling a stock that you were ethically opposed to or didn't believe in? Okay, now sell me that stock.

Special Information for MBAs

MBAs can expect two questions to carry the conversational exchange: "Tell me about yourself" and "Why are you interested in investment banking?" In this first round, recruiters are testing to see if you have the smarts to do the job and if investment banking is really your long-term goal. You're not being hired to build models for two or three years. The stakes are higher here. Remember that your past experiences don't necessarily determine your future, but you should at the very least be able to link the two. Think of it as a game of connect the dots. Look at your resume and try to create a splendidly logical progression from schools to previous jobs to outside interests to investment banking. You're allowed one anomaly—one dot that doesn't connect—but the rest should be excised. It's even better if you can show that your focus extends beyond investment banking to a particular industry or function—sales, M&A, or the oil and gas industry, for example.

This is also the interview in which they're likely to ask you to estimate the number of convenience stores in Manhattan or the number of golf balls that might fit in the room. We've discussed this already: You don't need to come up with an actual numeric answer, you just have to display masterful deductive reasoning skills. As a formality, you'll also probably be asked for your GPA, SAT, and GMAT scores. Rattle them off—accurately. Remember, there's a good chance that your record is in one of their folders and that they memorized it before you walked in the room.

One MBA recruiter on the CorpFin side says that, in addition, "You need to be prepared to value a company in a practical way, not just from a textbook, like you learned in business school." (See the "Review" section.) He says that, as with the brainteasers, "It's more important to demonstrate knowledge of the process. We aren't here to trip you up. Do some research, be prepared to answer questions about the company, and you'll be okay." He encourages doing some thorough homework on the firm you're interviewing with as well. "One guy obviously looked up our company on the Internet two months ago and didn't follow up so he had no idea of an important recent development." This recruiter advises candidates to "know what differentiates each firm from the next."

Candidates for sales and trading will go through similar first-round interview questions. Once again, it's all about "Why sales and trading?" and "Why you?" Keep in mind what we've discussed before: It's a bigger investment for traders to hire you because your costs come out of their pockets. Also, in training you, they're grooming a future competitor. While investment bankers are looking for diligent, likeable underlings who will follow directions and stay up all night, every night, traders need thick-skinned fireballs who have the potential to bring in the money as soon as possible. A high level of drive in these candidates
is critical.

Within S&T, it is important to know what you want to do and why. Fixed income is very different from equity; ditto sales and trading. If you say you are well suited for a variety of positions, first you'll be laughed at, then you'll be dinged. One sales and trading recruiter we spoke to confides, "Today I interviewed an undergraduate who I would classify as a disaster. I asked him, 'Why do you want to work on Wall Street?' He said he was interested in fixed income. Well, I really don't think this guy knew what fixed income was. He started to say that every day is exciting." The recruiter pauses and laughs. "Little did he know that often there are days when you go up to the trading floor and the traders are asleep at their desks because things are so slow. I think he just read *Liar's Poker* and romanticized the whole thing."

The same, but different. A current MBA associate recalls her first day of training, and how eager she was to meet this exclusive team that she had worked so hard to join. As it turned out, her peers were from surprisingly different professional and personal backgrounds. The only thing she could discern that this diverse group shared was an unyielding desire to work for this particular investment bank. That and a laundry list of accomplishments, each of which required drive, intelligence, and a commitment to excellence. During their short lifetimes, these players were all able to juggle a multitude of activities and always emerge out in front of everyone else. We asked recruiters to name some of the more unusual backgrounds they have encountered. With the caveat that investment banking associates "always have some previous experience in finance or a related industry," their list included a pro baseball player, a ballerina, an armed services officer, a buyer for a well-known fashion designer, a concert pianist, a PhD mathematician, a physicist, a pharmaceutical sales representative, and an Olympic athlete.

The Airplane Test

Every firm has a different term for the Could-I-Get-Along-with-this-Person? test. Some call it the "plane test." Interviewers ask themselves, "How would I feel sitting on an airplane or being delayed for hours in an airport with this person? Would it be okay? Better than okay? Or insufferable?"

Take, for example, Ralph. On paper Ralph is the perfect investment banking candidate: an Ivy Leaguer who worked as an analyst at another blue-chip investment bank prior to his acceptance at a top-tier MBA program, yada, yada, yada. Ralph has been invited to interview with five of the bulge-bracket firms. His resume screams, "Pick me!" However, in interview after interview, Ralph doesn't make the initial cut. Why? It's not because he isn't prepared; in fact, Ralph knows a lot about the business and has educated answers to every question. However, he never took seriously the fact that he has to pass the plane test.

Here's a pop quiz. Please circle all the gaffes you know Ralph is committing:

Ralph walks into his interview and presents a damp hand to the recruiter. (He'd visited the washroom just before his "conversation" and didn't stay through the end of the hot-air cycle.) "Yeah, fine," he responds to his female interviewer's pleasant "How are you?" He sits down before the recruiter does and looks out the window—not at her—stifling a yawn. She clearly notices the yawn. "Busy week," he offers gruffly, still not looking at her. He leans back in his chair, crosses his legs, and starts spinning his pen. She asks politely if he'd care for a cup of coffee to help him be more alert. "Sure," he replies, and remains seated while she leaves the room briefly for coffee.

When she returns, Ralph mumbles thanks and asks for more sugar. No "please." The recruiter complies (no "thank you," either) and then finally sits down and begins asking about Ralph's impeccable background. Like a well-rehearsed robot he walks her through his impressive resume. The recruiter follows up with, "How would your business school study group peers describe you, Ralph?" Ralph smirks and snaps his dollar-sign suspenders. "Definitely as a smart leader," he crows. ("Definitely as a smart-ass," she thinks.) "How would this guy take instruction from someone who is younger and more experienced?" she ponders. "And could I spend four hours waiting with this guy in an airport lounge?" She shudders.

In the interest of fairness, she gives Ralph a chance at the end of an interminable 25 minutes. "Are there any questions you would like to ask me, Ralph?" Long pause, after which Ralph replies, "No, I'm intimately familiar with the job, having been a successful analyst and all. But I see you're married," he adds, gesturing at her ring finger." "I bet you work so much you never see your husband, huh?" "Thanks for coming," she replies abruptly.

"I'm afraid that's all we have time for." Ralph leaves, confident this job is his for the asking. "See you at Super Saturday," he calls back over his shoulder as the next candidate is being ushered in.

Okay, hopefully you're not reading this thinking, "Seems like it all went well to me." Let's begin at the top. Dry, firm handshake and a cheerful greeting with eye contact are clearly mandatory. So are manners. Forget gender etiquette—you're younger (or even if you're not, you're currying favor) and you defer. Even if you're female and your interviewer is male, don't sit until he does. If the recruiter leaves the room for any reason, stand up when he or she returns. Do not yawn. Do not fiddle. Sit up straight. If you're offered something to drink, don't refuse—use this as an opportunity to accompany your interviewer and show how quietly helpful you can be. This will win a lot of points with recruiters and do a lot toward making your 30 minutes more memorable in their minds.

Next, if you can't convince yourself that your life is exciting and full of promise, Lord knows, no one else is going to be persuaded. Your resume needs to bedazzle bored interviewers. But how do your study group and other peers see you? To score points with this one, you must gracefully transform yourself into the picture of self-deprecating modesty. Pretend you're in a Japanese movie: The more esteemed the situation and the person you're addressing, the more humble pie you eat. Used with discretion (remember our discussion on humility?) this technique can work powerfully in your favor.

Continuing with Ralph's comedy of errors, no one in these politically correct times should be so boorish as to remark on someone's marital status. Additionally, one should never assume (explicitly or otherwise) that he or she is assured an invitation to a subsequent round of interviews. Furthermore, if you find yourself sitting across the table from someone you know or recognize, perhaps as a face you've seen on campus in the past or as someone who knows many of your friends, avoid any temptation to "get personal" or be informal. This is not the moment to renew old acquaintances. In the unlikely event the familiar face is willing to even acknowledge that he or she knows you, keep politeness uppermost in your mind.

Round 2 and Beyond

Unlike Reject Ralph, you made it. You did everything right (or at least nothing egregiously wrong). Now you're ready for Round Two. Most banks invite recruits to their New York headquarters for a grueling Friday night/Saturday/Saturday night of "socializing" and back-to-back interviews. (Some banks, however, also wedge in another round of interviews either in a hotel near your campus, a local branch of the firm, or New York City before the ordeal of Super Saturday.) From all reports, this further separating of wheat from chaff is very similar to the first round. The questions will be more focused, you'll be expected to know about the firm and your chosen line of work, and you will almost certainly have to repeat everything you said about yourself and your resume.

There are even ways to ensure that this repeat performance works to your advantage. If you're called back for either the interim round or Super Saturday, they're clearly interested. You might consider picking up the phone and asking your first-round interviewer for his or her suggestions on how you might improve your performance. However, you should only try this if you felt a real rapport with your first-round inquisitor and you know you can ask the right questions quickly and efficiently. If a recruiter whom you've never met calls to set up your second interview, do not grill him or her about your strengths and weaknesses. Bankers are busy, and if they've never met you, they can't help.

Several insiders were actually quite shocked when their interviewer called to congratulate them on reaching the next round and then offered unsolicited coaching on their interviewing style. One candidate says his interviewer noted that while he was a great candidate, he was a little too pushy and aggressive during the first round. Another student, considered very qualified but a bit unpolished, was coached on body language and appearance. If you are interviewing for a position in sales and trading, you may be relieved to hear that you will most likely never receive a courtesy coaching call before your final interview. Traders don't have time and, frankly, don't really care if you're shiny and polished.

P.S. The Walls Have Ears

The following true story illustrates a very simple rule we can't emphasize enough: Do not talk about your interview with other candidates, especially in the bathroom or the elevator. One morning an investment banking recruiter, clad in casual Friday attire, was taking the elevator up to her office for her first interview of the day. John and Mike, two prospective MBA candidates, were also in the elevator. Mike turned to John and asked with which part of the bank he was interviewing. Looking around the elevator and seeing only a few other people, none of whom looked like bankers, John replied, "Investment banking, but I'm actually not interested in this firm. I'm just doing it for practice." Ten minutes later, our recruiter went to meet her first candidate, who happened to be John. She greeted him politely and then told him there would be no interview. (We're not sure if John has figured out why yet.)

Friday Evening

You stayed up all last night finishing your term paper or wrapping up a case study, skipped lunch, and rushed to the airport to make your flight to New York, only to arrive in the Big Apple with one hour to spare. Anxiously you check into your swank midtown hotel and scamper off to the firm's "stop by and say hello" two-hour cocktail party. Dinner, with members of the firm who conveniently attended your alma mater, follows this rigorously formal "informal" social event. Keep in mind these people will be your strongest supporters if you impress them, for at most banks there is a lively internal competition among the folks from different schools. Also keep in mind that whenever there are representatives of the bank present, you need to think and act like you're selling yourself. (We know, this gets pretty tiring, but repetition is a very big part of this job. Might as well get used to it.)

Thus, regardless of your night-before activities (or inactivities, as the case may be), follow these few simple guidelines to ensure you're in prime condition the moment you step foot in the lobby of your travel benefactor. First, before you leave the hotel, eat something and drink some milk. People make much better entrances with blood sugar coursing at normal or heightened levels through their veins. For example, ballerinas usually pour honey down their throats or eat a banana before flinging themselves onstage.

When you enter the room, you have between one and two hours to meet, greet, and impress the sharks. Go. Before you head for the bar, keep in mind that every one of our insiders counsels against too much alcohol at this occasion (and any other where a managing director might be present). Don't forget that (a) this, too, is an interview, and (b) tomorrow morning you have a full day of "real" ones.

The way you handle yourself at these social gatherings is critical. Recruiters say that behavior at the cocktail parties and dinners is often their only way to assess how a future employee would act with a client. And while it's important to use this opportunity to introduce yourself to the senior people in the department you most want to work in, you also need to interact with the competition, plus the analysts and associates already in the slots you so desperately want. Recruiters pay a lot of attention to these group dynamics. Be sure you get a "plays well with others" on your sandbox report. When talking to the bankers, play things conservatively. No one likes a flirt or a suck-up, at least not in this situation. If you can't be completely, unaffectedly "yourself" (not easy in these circumstances, even for the gregarious and deeply secure), then follow the "two eyes, two ears, one mouth" rule: Watch and listen twice as much as you talk. Remember: It is much more important to attend politely to what others are saying than to dominate and dazzle the room with your wit and wisdom. After all, few clients would abide by a banker who refused to allow them to get a word in edgewise.

A seasoned MBA interviewer offers valuable advice: "Remember what your mother told you . . . take small bites and don't order salad or stringy noodles." You're on your first date, honey, and food that might end up on your teeth or your tie is food to avoid. Take small bites because someone will no doubt ask you a question the minute you start to swallow, and because mom's right, it makes a better impression on people. So does chewing quietly with your mouth closed, waiting for others to be served before you dig in, refraining from reaching even a short distance, and including the people on both your right and left in your conversation. It's also a good idea to refrain from jokes. Let others be the riotous wits at this function. We live in PC times, and you never know who you're going to offend. (When you actually go to work on a trading desk, you can be as sick and cynical and offensive as you please. But you're not there yet.)

P.S. Go to bed early. There's a reason it's called Super Saturday, and you'll need your beauty rest.

P.P.S. Before you pull up the covers, jot down the name of every person you can remember meeting and something about who they are and what part of the bank they work in. You'll be glad you did this tomorrow. Then, call the front desk and request a wake-up call. Then, go to sleep.

Social Gatherings . . .
From Cocktails to Lunch

Do

- Eat a snack or drink a glass of milk before cocktail hour.

- Seek out and introduce yourself to important players.

- Take small bites and use the cocktail napkins provided.

- Err on the side of being excessively polite.

- Respect the competition. With any luck, they will soon be your colleagues.

- Interact with your peers (and play well with others).

- Pay close attention to the name tags. Remember as many names as you can.

- Be yourself.

Don't

- Order messy hard-to-eat food.

- Eat fast or commit any other breach of table manners.

- Tell the latest dirty joke you heard.

- Be informal.

- Write down the name of everyone you meet in a notebook. (But, by all means, do it later.)

- Drink too much.

Your Final Interview

Good morning. You survived the previous night's social test and now it's time to come face-to-face with about six of those sharks, no longer holding drinks, no longer obliged to be nice to you. That's it, take off the fuzzy embossed robe, put on your starched shirt and neatly pressed dark suit, grab your leather-bound notepad, plus your names from last night, and move on out. It's Super Saturday. If it's any consolation, you're not the only one questioning the cruel euphemistic irony here. One insider comments ruefully on the nickname: "I hate referring to them as Super Saturdays. There is nothing super about any of the parties involved. I am missing my Saturday and the candidates are stressing their minds out."

Breakfast

You will most likely gather for breakfast with your peers and members of the firm in either a conference room or the corporate dining room before you're all sent off to meet the powers-that-be behind closed doors. Remember: As soon as you enter the breakfast room, your interview has begun. Recruiters admit that they do observe how candidates interact with their peers. Most say they are impressed with students who take initiative to greet their peers with a handshake and an introduction. (Try to remember, however, the ones you talked with, even briefly, yesterday. If they remember you, they'll want you to remember them.) Some official-looking person will hand you an interview schedule, which will list the senior-level bankers you'll be talking to and the groups in which they work.

Now it's time to sit down in a quiet corner and haul out your late-night jottings. Any names match up? Any desks and departments match up? If you had a nice chat with Mary Merger and Andy Acquisition at dinner, no harm in mentioning this when you go in to talk with their M&A bosses. Think about the topics they brought up and seemed interested in. These are the topics and questions in which you should be interested. Think about how they presented themselves and the firm. This is how you should present yourself. You were given a wealth of corporate and cultural information last night. Use it. Interviews will last anywhere from 30 minutes to one hour. If it makes you tired just thinking about it, wait until you have talked about yourself for five hours straight. This experience has been known to exhaust some of the biggest egos out there.

Pre-Game Warmups

Today the final decisions are made. Every person in the room is qualified and capable of doing the job, but not everyone will be given the chance. It is time to distinguish yourself from your peers. While round one was primarily about your ability to do the job, round two is more about assessing whether you would fit in at this firm. Why would you be better at a particular desk than all the others competing for the same slot? More importantly, do they like you? You need to be more polished, more focused, and have a clearer understanding of the business and the position than the other candidates. You also need to convey why you want to work for this firm, and only this firm. We are all reassured by others who seem like us. We are even more reassured if this person with whom we feel so comfortable validates our own splendid choice of employment. So be a chameleon and be as much like whomever you're talking to as possible. And make sure the subtext reads: If you like working here, I would obviously love working here. (Of course, remember that nugget of wisdom: To Thine Own Self Be True. A former analyst advises, "Every firm has its own culture, and anyone interviewing should stick to being themselves. Impress them, but be yourself. You really need to gauge if you're going to fit in or not. If you hate your interviewers, chances are you won't like their colleagues and you won't like the job. Pay attention.") All easier said than done, we grant you, but if you understand the intangibles, you can always make better use of them than if you don't.

Because you did your homework, you also know that each firm is a little different. Every corporate body has its own way of going about its business. One firm may like people who take initiative and think outside the box. Another may primarily assess your potential as a long-term banker. Are you a team player and a leader all wrapped into one? Can you intuit the moment when it is necessary to push others aside and grab the reins? Some firms may want you to leave that out-of-the-box thinking behind, conform, and just follow directions well. Do your research and know the preferences of the firm with which you're interviewing. One former analyst recalls, "The attitudes of my interviewers at Morgan Stanley and Wasserstein were vastly different. I now understand why I didn't get an offer from Morgan. I just didn't have the personality they were looking for. I guess I wasn't white-shoe enough. Thank God. I fit in much better at Salomon Smith Barney, where I ended up."

Welcome to the Show

Questions won't vary too much from those you were asked in the first round; there will just be more of them. Remember the resume connect-the-dots exercise? Now, more than ever, you need to make everything on there relate to investment banking—and to your interviewer and this particular firm. If you're interviewing for a summer associate position, it's particularly important to make a logical connection between what you did before business school and what you want to do both this summer and after graduation. Ignore the claim that recruiters don't really expect first-year MBAs to know what they want. Prepare as if they expect you to know. Choose an area and stick to it. If you are interviewing with sales and trading, do not mention that you are also considering corporate finance. Be specific about what you want to do in that area. S&T recruiters go nuts if you can't be intelligent about equity versus fixed income and why you want one over the other.

Each banker with whom you meet will have his or her own interviewing style. "Some of the guys wanted to push me to my limit and make me uncomfortable, while others just wanted to get to know me," says a recent hire. Consider yourself lucky if half the people you meet just want to engage you in a let's-get-acquainted chat, plus "Why do you want to be an investment banker?" and "How does your background make you suited to the job?" But you'll also probably encounter people bored and out of sorts (it is Saturday after all, and fairly early at that). They're ready to take this out on you and test your quantitative intelligence and survival instincts. It's best to admit that you do not know an answer right off the bat, and feel stupid for a split second, than to pretend and get caught. If an interviewer senses that you're pretending to understand something, he or she will likely push you until you break. An insider who has had countless investment-banking interviews says, "When you don't know, say you don't know. Just remember you should never have to say it twice." Being a chameleon means ceding control. Let the interviewer control what's going on here. You need to appear competent, but not in charge.

Interview Prep Exercise

Study your resume. What have you done or studied that coincides with what recruiters are looking for? Find examples in which you demonstrated leadership, dedication, success under pressure, an ability to juggle priorities, quantitative analysis ability, and teamwork. You also need to find whatever the firm was plugging hardest at that first campus information session. If they care about X, you care about X.

_____

_____

_____

_____

_____

_____

In one minute, maybe two, try to logically link the experiences on your resume to one another and then to your future in investment banking. Rather than list the skills, demonstrate them through examples. Why would you be a successful analyst/associate/trader/salesperson? How do you exemplify how this firm already sees itself? (In other words, if the firm touts global, how can you appear to be international?)

_____

_____

_____

_____

_____

_____

who you're trying to convince with this pitch. (If it is you, our career choice.) Knowing your audience is key. HR staff n to be predominantly female. They usually drag a male along h one is senior? This isn't sexist; it's just real life. Pitch to the one who's in charge. You may have no way of knowing in advance, so best prepare two spiels.

_____

_____

_____

_____

_____

_____

_____

_____

_____

_____

_____

_____

_____

_____

_____

_____

_____

_____

_____

_____

_____

_____

_____

A Few Words on the Stress Interview

A young man enters the interview room cautiously and, remembering all the advice he's heard, greets his interviewer politely and sits down only after he's asked to. His interviewer then proceeds to whip out a newspaper and immerse himself in it. One minute passes, five, ten. . . . The candidate remains poised anxiously on his chair, waiting for the interview to begin. Finally after 20 minutes, the interviewer folds up his paper, turns to the baffled, silent candidate and announces that the interview is over. "You're obviously not aggressive enough," he says. "You wouldn't be the type of person who would succeed at our firm."

Stress Interview? You Be the Judge.

People engaged in a word-association game might instinctively blurt out "stress interviews" when they hear the trigger "investment banking." Tactics popular back in the '70s continue to be told as war stories. Ask anyone and they'll tell you about the candidate who spent ten minutes trying to open a window that had deliberately been nailed shut. Even more widely told is the two-on-one, good-cop/bad-cop interview where the candidate leaves so stressed out she doesn't even care if she got the job. While times and tactics have changed, stress interviews continue. The newspaper is no longer enough of a surprise. And most Manhattan skyscraper windows are permanently sealed shut, as even the most gullible undergrad knows. Nowadays, your interviewer will just sit there in silence and wait for you to take the initiative to start selling yourself. Or he'll bark out the famous 15 cheeseburger orders and tell you to hop to.

A former analyst recounts this story: "In my interview, the guy focused on the fact that I had played in a band in college. Of course I had listed that I played bass guitar, but he wanted to see if I had more talents. He then proceeded to conference in four other guys and then made me sing a few lines of a song. I'm tone deaf, but I did it. Granted, I was extremely embarrassed but for some reason they thought it was funny and seemed pleased. How's that for induced stress?"

Bankers and recruiters define stress interviews rather differently from prospective candidates. When asked if investment banks employ stress interviews, all of our banking sources insist that they do not, yet most every recent interviewee with whom we spoke says, "Of course." One recruiter offers a rationalization for this interpretive divergence: "We discourage them. However, it's important to remember it's all perception. A candidate may have a different notion of what a stress tactic is than a banker. Just because he or she is unprepared does not mean we are deliberately trying to evoke stress."

While no one can prepare for every wild pitch, make sure you know what's expected of you in general terms. If this is a job that requires aggressive sales, in the face of all odds, be aggressive and sell. There will always be the random banker who just wants to make you uncomfortable. Sometimes you can best these types, but more often, you can't. Just take a few deep breaths and roll with the punches. More often than not, your ability to keep your wits about you through the entire encounter is all that's being tested in a stress interview. For your edification and amusement, we will share with you some of our favorite '90s war stories:

- A former analyst recalls an interview in which a woman, not much older than she, looked at her without so much as a smile and said, "Okay, tell me a joke. Entertain me for five minutes and then we'll see if I want to stay and learn more about you." (Note: Under no circumstances is this an invitation to serve up an off-color joke. Keep it clean and non-discriminatory. If your repertoire doesn't include anything appropriate, add to it before you show up for these rounds.)

- In one "good cop/bad cop" interview, a candidate became so infuriated by Mr. Bad Cop's harsh interrogation and obvious scorn, she threw caution to the wind and began giving as good as she got. Convinced she'd nixed any chance of ever getting a job on Wall Street, she arrived home to a phone call from the bad cop inviting her back for a second round of interviews the following morning. He made a point of congratulating her on her assertiveness and her ability to handle pressure. (Remember: Keep your wits.)

- Another insider remembers the banker who wouldn't shut up for the majority of the interview, and out of politeness, our source thought it best not to interject. At the end of the session, the banker criticized him for his lack of assertiveness.

- One interviewer came right to the point: "I see you're smart, have worked hard, have a nice tan. But what I really want to know is, can you add value? Or, at least, can we teach you?"

Regardless of the questions asked and the tactics employed by an interviewer, keep in mind you are being assessed on how you handle "a situation." (There's a reason they call that special room in the White House basement "the situation room.") Stay cool and be prepared for anything. One undergraduate candidate arose Super Saturday morning feeling a bit queasy. In an effort to calm his tossy tummy, he ate a little breakfast and set off for the firm. With all the glowing adjectives his coworkers, dog, family, and teammates might use to favorably describe him spinning in his head, he started up in the elevator to the 30th floor. The doors opened and before our candidate could greet his peers and recruiters, most of whom were standing less than ten feet away, he threw up all over the floor. Instant gong, right? Actually, he handled the situation so well that, after returning for another Super Saturday, he received and accepted an offer—and the affectionate office nickname "Chuck."

Your Turn to Ask the Questions

The interview is drawing to a close. You're almost there. The recruiter or banker has asked if you have any questions or feel there is something of importance to you that was not touched upon during your discussion. Whatever you do, this is not a cue to sit back, cross your legs, and relax. Insiders say that this is the point where many strong candidates talk their way into a rejection letter. First, don't feel obligated to ask a question. If it comes out sounding canned, you'll be dinged even as you speak. A current MBA student with several outstanding offers explains that he uses the question time to close the interview and sum up his candidacy. He suggests: "Thanks. I think you've probably answered all my important questions, but I would like to leave you with three things to consider about my candidacy. . . ."

Recruiters say that candidates can lose points by asking meaningless questions whose only purpose is to prove they read the *Wall Street Journal* that morning, or, worse, repeating something that's already been discussed. A quick way to get dinged is to ask an academic or abstruse sort of question, which has no straightforward answer, just to show how clever you are. If you think you have a good question and would honestly like it answered, ask it and include, whenever possible, qualifiers that show how thoroughly you've researched the firm. For example: "I know you've moved a lot of people around in the past year, both here and in your West Coast branches, and there also appear to have been some fairly significant management changes at the senior executive levels. But I'm still curious as to why your rating dropped 24 points in the *Fortune* '100 Best Places to Work.' These factors explain some, but perhaps not all, of what happened. Would you mind talking about this a bit more?"

Even if they hate answering this question, your interviewers will give you top marks for having done your homework—and also for giving them some ways out they might not have thought of on their own. How attentively you listen to their response also makes a difference. If they parrot back to you the easy out you just gave them, save your skepticism for the moment you have an offer in hand. Nod your head, look interested, lean forward slightly, and let them off the hook if they start to visibly squirm. They don't like answering tough questions any more than you do.

Last-Minute Comebacks—and Surprises

It's the bottom of the ninth, two outs, runner on first, and you're trailing by a run. You're at the plate. It's up to you. Feeling like you want to give up? Don't! There still may be room for a comeback. Not a lot, but you can do it. A few recruiters from top-tier firms confirm that last-minute comebacks do occur. Sometimes. An interview is so short and the interviewers tend to be so seasoned that they form an impression of a candidate's competency and fit within the first five minutes. Thus, a comeback is more likely to occur shortly after these initial minutes rather than three-quarters of the way through the interview. One insider reveals: "One guy was so lackluster in the first two minutes, I thought, 'oh, yuck.' But then he got it going and by the end, I really thought he'd be a great candidate. . . . This is pretty rare. The best candidates tend to be consistent from the minute they step in my office to the minute they leave." The reverse is also possible: Some candidates come on strong in the beginning but then get too comfortable. It all comes down to that dreaded casual behavior.

Finally, never assume that at any point in the interview you're home free. One insider says, "My last interviewer stood up and thanked me for coming. I followed suit and was relieved that it was over and my heart could finally slow down to a normal pace. I was confident that I was well on my way to an offer when all of a sudden, two other bankers charged into the room. 'Have a seat,' one of them ordered. 'This interview is far from over.' For the next 45 minutes, these two guys grilled me like there was no tomorrow. After I received an offer, I learned that as a candidate gets closer to the brass ring, the firm will sometimes tighten up just to see how he or she reacts to some unexpected pressure."

In Summation

If you had to leave your interviewer with three thoughts about you, what would they be? Fill in answers to the following questions to help you refine your pitch and remind you of the thoughts you want to leave with your interviewer.

What distinguishes you from your peers?

_____

_____

_____

_____

_____

_____

Why would you be a particularly good candidate for this job?

_____

_____

_____

_____

_____

_____

📄 In Summation . . . continued

How could you add value?

_____

_____

_____

_____

_____

_____

_____

How do your past accomplishments show that you can do the job?

_____

_____

_____

_____

_____

_____

_____

Your responses to these questions provide an interviewer with four reasons the bank should hire you. Choose the three strongest. Try not to forget them the next time.

Denouement

You survived seven grueling interviews and you're ready to cozy up next to the fire with a hot cup of cocoa to relax your aching brain and sore facial muscles. Unfortunately, your travel benefactors have other plans in store. While the interviewers convene to share their thoughts and impressions, you'll be whisked off to a fancy Manhattan restaurant or the firm's corporate dining room for an "informal" lunch or dinner with either analysts or associates who already hold the job for which you yearn. As you know, the word "informal" is utterly bogus; your dining companions will still be gathering intelligence on the weary candidates.

If you are an undergraduate, consider yourself lucky. These gatherings are mostly just a chance to question analysts who currently hold one of the coveted positions you so desperately want. But for MBAs, the lunch, or whatever follows the interview ordeal, is a time to interact with future colleagues, and the "client test" is still in effect. One insider says, "Your behavior at lunch most likely won't affect their decision unless you really screw up. But speaking as someone who had to go to those lunches, certain questions and jokes turned me off, and when the person started in the fall I did not forget them." On one occasion, a prospective candidate who had all but clinched an offer managed to offend nearly every other candidate and current employee at the table. He apparently not only ate like a horse, but also attacked the small number of women and minorities in the program, and then proceeded to act condescendingly toward the other candidates. Not surprisingly, he got the gong.

Another insider tells of a candidate who was a shoo-in for an offer until they all went out for dinner. "We were at the Penn Club after a long day of interviews, and this guy proceeded to get really drunk on grasshopper shots and 19 other ridiculous drinks. My first thought was, not only is he an idiot, but how could we trust him with clients? Could you imagine what his expense report would look like? It was inevitable that he'd take advantage of the system if he already had the gall to do it before he even landed the job."

The Offer

You got the call. They want you. The judging is over and now the firm wants last week's outsider to be a permanent insider. Celebrity status begins here. You are invited to New York for some wining, dining, and, if you're lucky, even a little dancing. A current analyst or associate will be assigned to be your buddy. He or she will become your new best friend and information source. The info and friendship are obviously a bit suspect and it's important not to let too much of this go to your head. The judging is not over, friend. How you handle the offer will be remembered.

A former analyst recalls his "sell night" dinner. "Fun was flowing everywhere. I never felt like such a celebrity. Things were great until one guy, who I quickly realized was smashed, turned to a recruiter and told her a joke derogatory towards homosexuals. The joke-teller's laughter was reverberating off the thick silence and wide-eyed stares of everyone seated at the table." Apparently the offer held (sometimes it's actually rescinded), but as our source notes, "This behavior sure didn't win him any points when it came time for group selection."

Insiders confirm there are definite right and wrong ways to handle an offer. One recruiter says, "How you handle an offer reflects a lot about you. We've had people handle the acceptance so poorly I wish they hadn't [received an offer]. Watch out, because you can piss people off and they won't want to work with you." Whatever you do, don't lie about offers from other firms. This will come back to haunt you. Especially in the case of summer associates, recruiters often call around to other firms to see who else has offers out to a particular student. (Remember: Wall Street is like a small town.)

When is the best time to accept? Many of us believe that if we say "yes" too quickly, we'll appear desperate and less desirable. Some may think that if you make them wait, they'll want you more and therefore pay you more. Puh-leaze! Let's keep things in perspective here. No one is asking you to run the company. They need you, sure, but several hundred, in some cases thousands, of eager applicants would kill for this spot, and the firm knows it even if you don't. If you accept an investment banking offer on the spot, it may actually work to your benefit. For example, if you know at the outset you want very much to work for a particular group, or, in the case of S&T hires, after your training period you hope to land at a particular desk, the powers-that-be will usually remember. In some cases, it may even be advantageous to state in your interview that if given an offer, you would accept on the spot. Of course, then you obviously absolutely have to. You won't have free will for a whole lot longer. Think seriously before giving it up.

Think even more seriously before pulling a fast one. Or playing one firm too long and hard against another. "They think they can screw us," says one recruiter, "but they don't realize that we can screw them, too. Wall Street is not that big." One insider remembers a senior managing director extending an offer to a student for a trader position and reiterating that he was only going to offer once. No ritual mating dance, just "yes" or "no." The student gave him very positive feedback (interpreted as "yes") and then accepted a position with another firm. Unfortunately for the candidate, the director had lots of pals at the rival firm (of course he did—they all do) and he logged a quick call to explain the situation. You know the end of this story. You also know its moral: Big hitters in big positions have big friends in big positions. Moreover, they have equally big egos. They're not called Masters of the Universe for nothing. So be careful.

Dealing With the Offer

Do

- Be honest about why you need to extend the acceptance date. If you have a legitimate reason, most recruiters will be flexible. They abided by your school's deadlines set up to protect you and give you ample time to interview. You now need to abide by theirs. A firm might give preferential treatment to a former star analyst, but in general everyone is treated equally.

- Foster an open discussion if you have offers from more than one firm. "I am excited about your offer but am honestly leaning towards XYZ firm." Let them woo you. Especially if they made your life miserable during one or more stress interviews.

- Be fair. If you accept and then pull out at the last minute, you're taking a spot away from someone who probably really wants to be there.

- Accept on the spot if you know this firm is really where you want to work.

- Do your homework and think hard about where you'd be most happy. Do this with equal parts left and right sides of the brain. In other words, ignore earnings for a moment and focus on vibes. One MBA student admits that he didn't accept a very prestigious offer because he felt endlessly tripped up during the interview process.

Don't

- Tell a recruiter you have another offer when you don't. They'll check. And then you'll be sorry.

- Request an extension because you'll be on vacation until after the acceptance deadline date or for any other unimportant personal reason. This does not win you points.

- Accept a job at a firm just because of its brand name. Pay attention to the culture. You're going to be spending a lot of time in that building. Make sure you like just about everything there is to like about it.

Salary Negotiations

Fact: Most of us hate haggling about money. Very few people are good at it. If you'd like some guidelines as to how to do it better, we suggest reading the WetFeet Insider Guide *Negotiating Your Salary and Perks*. Also worthwhile is the well-known negotiation guide, *Getting to Yes: Negotiating Agreement Without Giving In*, by Roger Fisher and William Ury.

Regardless of your salary negotiation prowess, analysts and associates don't have much room to maneuver here. Every few years, one of the bulge brackets ups the starting salaries $5–10K and all the other investment banks scramble to bring their own offers into line. For example, in '96 and '97, Goldman inched the industry standard base salary up to approximately $40,000 per year for undergrads and $75,000 for MBAs. It also began tacking on signing bonuses— very uncommon previously—of up to $25,000 to woo the best and brightest. A fair number of others felt obliged to follow suit. So, unless you're coming in at a more senior level or with considerably more experience than most of your peers, the numbers are rigid. You can't change them.

That said, you can occasionally negotiate reimbursement of relocation costs and assistance for spouses or significant others, but part of the rationale behind the signing bonus is to cover these and other expenses.

While the base salary for incoming analysts and associates may seem lower than what your management consultant pals get, bask in the knowledge that you're pretty much guaranteed a year-end bonus and they aren't. Your first-year bonus can range anywhere from 20 to 50 percent of your base salary—and that's only the start. Work hard, make some significant contributions, gain some visibility, and generate some goodwill, and your 20 percent can easily reach 100 percent by the end of your third year.

Interview Workbook

- Sample Q&A

- I-Banking vs. Management Consulting

- Never Let Down Your Guard

- Q&A Thought Balloons

Sample Q&A

You've churned through every paragraph of this page-turner. You know the sections of the investment bank like the back of your hand, you understand the philosophy of the interviewers, and you're confident that you have what it takes to really excel in this environment. But, wait! You're still a little edgy about the interview questions that you'll have to field. Well, to help you navigate your way through those interviews, we've collected questions from interviewees, discussed the appropriate answers with interviewers, and put together a short list of leading questions and recommended answers. Remember, there often are no "right" answers—a particular interviewer may have a different approach from somebody else at the same firm. However, based on our research, you should definitely anticipate certain questions. The following pages contain those and WetFeet's comments about how to approach them. Space for your own responses follows that.

CorpFin—Analysts

Interviewer: What is the role of an investment bank?

WetFeet: Many undergraduates interviewing for analyst positions don't have a clue what investment banks do. Understanding the difference between some of the basic financial products and the ability to confidently explain what an investment bank does will make you stand out. (For a quick-and-dirty synopsis of the investment banking industry, check out WetFeet's Insider Guide to Careers in Investment Banking.) If you can then further define the role of Bank X, the one you most want to work for, and how it differs from its chief competitors, you will be a star.

An investment bank provides financial advisory services to corporations government institutions... They advise on the best way to raise capital whether thru debt or equity offerings. In which the bank helps the company determine a price, buys the securities and then resells them to investors (spread) at a higher price. An invest bank also provides advice on topics such mergers and acquisitions, or investment strategies. From my understanding it is the go to when corporations and institutions are seeking to raise capital and when investors want to buy, sell or trade securities.

Interviewer: Are you prepared to work 80 hours per week, and how have you ever exhibited such dedication in the past?

WetFeet: Have at least one, preferably several, examples ready of projects and passions you have cheerfully devoted at least this much time to in the past. They're looking for drive and commitment. Show them you have both in abundance. Probably correctly, dedication is seen as easily transferable.

Interviewer: Why would you be a good analyst?

WetFeet: If you make it clear to the interviewer that you understand an analyst's responsibilities, then you'll have a much easier time employing your seemingly unrelated skills for the building and analyzing of models, the researching of competitors, the meticulous checking of pitch books, or whatever the job entails. As in any industry, if you can talk the talk, your credibility skyrockets.

From my research a good analyst is someone who is good with numbers, motivated, focused on learning, can ~~han~~ multi-task, analytica[l]. As economics major most of my course work involves numbers and analysis so I'm definitely comfortable with both. For example in my Econometric class for the final project my partner and I were looking at ~~the~~ how different factors affected American earnings. Which involved numbers about average income, # of children and so forth. After we got the relationships between Income and those factors we had to analyze what the numbers meant and determine possible reasonings for why we got those numbers particularly if they were inconsistent with our hypothesis (work exp was neg)

Multi-tasking, I think part of being a college student is multi-tasking. I go to school full-time and work part-time. Sometimes I find myself having to juggle diff projects for different classes and still having to find time to attend group meetings. But like I said it's part of being a college student.

Interviewer: What is your greatest weakness?

WetFeet: Once again, if you can analyze yourself and manage to put a positive "I have learned from this" spin on it, you have answered correctly. Those of you who see this as the moment for an honest "I'm not good with numbers" confession, think again. Recruiters are by no means expecting you to come clean. In fact, this question is posed more to discern whether you have prepared and whether you can "maturely" assess yourself. If asked to list your strengths, be sure to pick ones that the firm wants their analysts to possess.

Public Speaking is my greatest weakness. I get nervous having to talk infront of a crowd. However, I realize that Public speaking is not something I could run from no matter what my profession. So I'm trying to get over that fear slowly but surely. For instance for group presentations I have to speak infront of my class there is no way around it. And it is actually becoming less nervous. I even volunteered to speak infront of a crowd for a college expedition held in St. Kitts. I wasn't expecting that many people but there was a turn-out of over 300 people. I did my presentation and it went well. So I'm definitely working on my Public Speaking weakness

Interviewer: Where else are you interviewing?

WetFeet: This is not another invitation for a true confession. If you are interviewing with consulting firms, consumer product companies, and sports marketing firms, mum's the word. We don't recommend lying—a real no-no in any interview—but we don't encourage full disclosure, if it will make you seem unfocused and tactless. (And farther down the road, tact and discretion count for as much as stamina in your early years.) Your interviewers expect you to say you only want to be a banker and therefore you are solely concentrating your job hunt in the industry. List their chief competitors and then shut up. Do not volunteer, "Well, of course, an M&A job with your firm is my first choice, but I'm also talking to Salomon Smith Barney about a trading job and to CSFB about a research job." Remember, a focused message is important. Don't take this as an invitation to compare this bank with others.

Interviewer: What course did you most enjoy in college?

WetFeet: Enthusiastic as you may have been about the theater workshop you took last year, this would be a bad answer. (The only possible exception might be for sales or trading, but you had better be able to connect some fairly distant dots.) Instead, think about what this investment bank does (or likes to think it does) best and find a relevant course. If your bank is going after emerging markets, the semester you spent studying Asian governments is a fine choice. In other words, you don't have to say Accounting 101. But whatever you do choose, make sure you got a reasonably good grade in it and you remember enough to discuss it intelligently.

_____

_____

_____

_____

_____

_____

_____

_____

_____

_____

_____

_____

_____

_____

_____

_____

_____

_____

_____

_____

Interviewer: Why our firm? Compare us to Goldman or Merrill. (Or, if you're at one of these two, you'll be asked to compare the firm to Morgan Stanley or Citigroup.)

WetFeet: This is a thinly disguised "Have you done your research?" question. It's also a test to see if you can be both honest and sycophantic while appearing to be only the former. Why do you like the firm? Talk about the great people you've met and how impressed you were that they spent the time they did educating you about the firm. How appreciative you were that they bothered to call you after your interviews and coach you for the next round. Or whatever. Don't make anything up, but don't refrain from putting a favorable spin on actual events. For example, if you called first and they called back with lots of helpful coaching, give them all the credit. It is also critical that you be able to differentiate the firm's culture without putting down its competitors. Tell your interviewers what they want to hear. If ethics are of overriding importance at this firm, they are of overriding importance to you. If this is a firm with lots of contrarian views, that's you. Most important, stroke your interviewer's ego whenever possible. For example, whatever they're best at, you want to be at the firm that does that thing better than anyone else.

Firstly, Goldman Sachs one of the largest securities bank and considered the best investment bank on the Street. Of course, the learning experience wd be similar no matter which bank I go to, so it ultimately boils down to the people and the culture. There I've me been honored to meet great people from analysts to Managing Directors and I always, take away a sense of camaraderie. It is important to me to know that I would be working with people who want to help me achieve greatness. Having employees take time out to email me back about interviewing tips and having been afforded the opportunity to fly to NY at the expence of Goldman to meet employees and receive insider tips speaks alot about the firm and its efforts to invest in people who cando great things. From research and infosessions the culture at Goldman seems to be really elevated on teamwork and helping each other out as opposed every man for himself

CorpFin—Associates

The questions for associates are similar from round to round. While you are charming them with your dazzling personality and team spirit, don't let them forget that you're hungry for this job and you really like both the work and the firm. You are being prepped to live in the long-term banker box so sell yourself accordingly. As an MBA associate, you are required to be both a team player and a potential leader. How? Just keep in mind that leadership is the ability to get extraordinary achievement from ordinary people. And since most of banking is done in groups, a leader's success is inextricably tied up in the output of his or her team. While the majority of the questions will be relatively straightforward probes into your ethics, business savvy, and general self-awareness, be prepared for the random bond-math question. The following pages contain some typical questions that recruiters ask.

Interviewer: What might a study group peer say your strengths and weaknesses are?

WetFeet: This question is designed to test your self-awareness. It also tests the all-important How Well You Work On Teams (HWYWOT). If you understand the role you typically play in group situations and have a reasonably accurate grasp of how others see you, this bodes well for HWYWOT. One recruiter says she always wants to hear that candidates are flexible: While at times they might coordinate activities, at others, they should demonstrate comfort and assurance with sitting back and taking instruction from those who are more knowledgeable. If you can recognize the appropriate time to step up to the plate and swing, banks will love you. The same recruiter notes that if a candidate claims to be a leader all the time, his or her HWYWOT score plummets. "There is no way they will be able to take direction once on the job," she says.

_____

_____

_____

_____

_____

_____

_____

_____

_____

_____

_____

_____

_____

_____

_____

_____

_____

Interview Workbook

Interviewer: If our firm didn't exist, which firm would be at the top of your list and why?

WetFeet: One insider claims that this question, more often than not, reveals a candidate's true colors. (The follow-up question, of course, is "But since we do exist, why did you choose us?") Our source says, "If they cannot intelligently answer why they chose our firm over their second choice then I question their interest level, not to mention whether they have really researched the firm."

_____

_____

_____

_____

_____

_____

_____

_____

_____

_____

_____

_____

_____

_____

_____

_____

_____

_____

_____

_____

_____

_____

Interviewer: Why do you want to be an investment banker?

WetFeet: Insiders agree the worst response to this question is, "Because I want to do deals and make money." What does that say about you? Nothing. A better answer would be something about your background that clearly predisposes you to running Excel till your eyes twirl. There is no perfect "right" answer, but sincerity is important here. The strangest answer? Probably the candidate who insisted the best part of the job would be the lucite tombstones many firms hand out at the successful completion of an underwriting. (It is clear from our research that most recruiters do not subscribe to wry and ironic wit. If you're going to be clever, skip the irony.)

Interviewer: Please value XYZ Company.

WetFeet: This is one of the most important questions for which you can prepare. When an interviewer asks you to value a particular company, be ready to walk him or her through your answer efficiently but also with a bit of flair. Stay away from the textbook answers, for they often come across as canned and the interviewer will question your grasp of the concept. And though textbooks and other sources are a fine beginning for your prep work, they generally can't give you enough material to deflect the curve balls many interviewers like to lob at you mid-valuation. As with brainteasers and case questions, these folks need to be reassured you understand the process; the quantitative data of the valuation matter less. See "Valuing a Company" for more detailed information about how to handle these questions.

_____

_____

_____

_____

_____

_____

_____

_____

_____

_____

_____

_____

_____

Interviewer: Please discuss a deal you have worked on in the past and your role in the transaction.

WetFeet: A word to any of you resume-padders out there: If you cite a deal on your resume, make sure you know the details backward and forward. Interviewers invariably ask candidates to explain key drivers behind the deal, the structure, the fees, and the rationale behind the choice of financing. Watch out for EBITDA multiples. Recruiters know they trip people up, and they're merciless. Forewarned is forearmed.

_____

_____

_____

_____

_____

_____

_____

_____

_____

_____

_____

_____

_____

_____

_____

_____

_____

_____

_____

_____

Sales & Trading—Analysts and Associates

These recruiters really do not expect undergrads to know much. Questions will focus more on your quantitative abilities, personality, and whatever that elusive intangible is that makes for great salespeople and traders. One recruiter says that these interviews tend to be more benign because the various desks know they'll be training candidates from day one. You need to have potential; your greatest weakness and favorite course are not important.

If you're an MBA or prospective summer intern, the stakes are a bit higher. Round two is usually very similar to round one except that this time you meet many more sharks. Time is money for these folks. Ask intelligent questions, show that you know the markets and this bank's products, keep your sentences short, and go ahead and use your hands and facial expressions more than you would in investment banking. This is all about getting along with large egos who have created a raw, in-your-face work environment. They're looking for quick-thinking, confident, thick-skinned risk-takers.

If you're after an S&T position, prepare for the questions on the following pages.

Interviewer: Demonstrate your sales skills: Sell me this desk.

WetFeet: This is not a cue to detail your previous sales experiences, nor to extol impressive financial sales techniques you've read about. Rather, it's an invitation to roll up your neatly pressed shirt sleeves and give them the quick 30-second hard sell. For those of you who don't have any experience in sales, we suggest you structure your pitch something like this:

- What kind of desk do you use now?

- What do like about it? What would you change?

- If you had an ideal desk what features would it have?

- May I suggest then that you check out this desk?

Do all this with as deft a combination of serious purposefulness and good humor as you can muster. The clear message to your interviewer has to be: I know this is a goof, but don't worry, I also know what you're looking for and I can deliver, even on goofs.

Interviewer: Which are you interested in, equity or fixed income, and why?

WetFeet: The two are quite different and if you're still not sure why or which you prefer, do some reading and talk to people who understand both. Once you've formulated an opinion, be sure to convey it convincingly. Also be sure to link any related previous job experience to your choice. If you know something about commercial credit because you once worked in a bank, use it in your pitch for an equity job. Or go for the historical rationale. You want fixed income because ever since 1979 and Paul Volcker's "intentional" recession and Carter's "deregulation" of interest rates, bonds have been more interesting and in many ways more volatile than equities. Interviewers like it a lot when callow youth can demonstrate some understanding of the distant past. (Now go do the homework so you really know what we're talking about here.)

Interviewer: Which do you want, sales or trading? Why?

WetFeet: Once again, these two are very different, and if you don't know how or why, you need to. A good answer for why you want to work in trading might be: "I'm pretty good at reading subtexts—through people's body language, voice intonation, what they don't say when they're talking about money. I learned a lot of this at my job at [you fill in the blank], but I also just seem to have a knack for it. I can almost always tell when someone is bluffing." Or if you want to work in sales: "I like people and they seem to like me. They seem to trust me, even though I'm often younger than they are. When I had [job X], I learned to use this in ways that helped me a lot in selling. I'm also probably not enough of a gambler to be a good trader. Doing the best job for a customer matters a lot more to me." Traders are a lot closer to the real money and the real risks than sales. If this excites you, say so. If it makes you even a little nervous, steer a middle course but be aware that this is a reality you need to address.

Other Favorite Questions

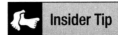

In the interest of leaving no stone unturned, here are some other interview favorites that might arise during your "conversations" with recruiters from any of the areas of investment banking—CorpFin, S&T, or Research. Again, play to your audience. This is not an Encounter Group moment.

- How well do you handle surprises? Give me an example.

- How do you feel about wealth?

- Teach me something unrelated to banking.

- Name three adjectives your roommate, family, best friend, colleague, or employer would use to describe you.

- Tell me your biggest accomplishment. (Hint: Tie it into the strengths they seem to look for at this firm.)

- Tell me about a difficult project you handled.

- Career changers: Please tell me how your previous job experience led you to this company.

- Give examples of projects you have done in which you used the same skills as you will use in this job.

- Where do you see yourself in five years?

- Do you prefer working on a team or alone?

- If you could do anything, what would you do? (Easy: "This job." Try to make it sound sincere. If you can't, be honest but think of lots of ways it links to "this job.")

- Tell me about the most interesting job you have had.

- Give me an example of your leadership ability. (Or, What kind of manager are you?)

- Please describe more thoroughly X experience listed on your resume.

- What do you think your favorite part of the job will be?

I-Banking vs. Management Consulting

Thinking about consulting *and* investment banking? Although both bankers and consultants know that many top students are interviewing with both industries, it's probably best to avoid pointing out that you're talking to the other side. At a minimum, don't yammer on about it—you'll look clueless and unfocused and you may earn yourself a ding. The recruiting processes for both are competitive and intense, but based on our conversations with recruiters from both sides, here are some of the differences.

Consulting Firms

- Are apt to interview candidates in the office they're applying to.

- Like "Do you fit our culture?" questions, but these may account for about 50 percent of the interview and decision.

- Love case questions focused on business operations (e.g., "Why are the profits for company X going down, when revenues are rising?").

- Look for candidate's ability to analyze a problem and deduce an answer.

- Typically push candidate to the conclusion of the case question and often ask for implications and recommendations.

- Tend to be fairly friendly (although the case questions can be nerve-racking).

- Love quantitative skills, but also seek people who have strong presentation and people skills.

- Look for strong interest in business.

- Look for stamina.

Investment Banking Firms

- Hire through the corporate headquarters, where the majority of employees work (generally Manhattan).

- Love "Do you fit our culture?" questions, which account for perhaps 75 percent of the decision.

- Tend to focus on hypothetical questions involving valuation, financing strategy, and markets.

- Pay more attention to candidate's process in deriving the answer (e.g., building the model) than to the actual quantitative solution.

- Often cut candidates off mid-sentence once it's apparent they know a practical way to solve a problem.

- Hold interviews that can be more confrontational, or designed to create pressure on the candidate.

- Look for strong sales skills, particularly in sales and trading.

- Look for strong interest in finance.

- Look for exceptional stamina and drive.

Never Let Down Your Guard

Questions that on first impression seem irrelevant rarely are. There is almost no such thing as an unimportant or meaningless question in an investment banking interview. If you are presented with any such queries (a few of which we set forth below), use the opportunity to reveal your personality and your outside interests. Remember not to come across as too self-absorbed. For example, if a particular question affords you an opportunity to introduce your passion for marathoning, it's appropriate to let your interviewer know that you train, say, 30 miles a week. But don't disclose (even if it's true) that you have to run by yourself because you can't possibly run with other people. And stay away from controversial areas like politics and religion. You are not talking to your shrink, and soul-searching truth has a low priority here. Below are several more examples of oft-asked disarming queries and suggested good and bad responses.

Interviewer: If you were stranded on a desert island for one year, what three people would you want with you?

Good answers

- The former company director who now investigates misdeeds for the SEC
- Paul Bunyon (or some other hearty, outdoorsy, "can-do" type)
- Alice of Alice's Restaurant

Bad answers

- Arch-rival and foe's former partner who now runs the Fed
- Gilligan (or Tina Louise)
- Martha Stewart

Interviewer: If you could have any job besides banking what would it be?

Good answer: Concert pianist

Bad answer: Accountant

Interviewer: What is the last book you read (or What is your favorite book?)

Good answers

- *Jane Eyre*
- *The Way Things Work*
- Eliot Janeway's *The Economics of Imperialism*

Bad answers

- Stephen King's *The Stand*
- *The Joy of Cooking*
- Michael Lewis' *Liar's Poker*

Interviewer: What did you do last weekend?

Good answers:

- Went skiing with friends
- Read two books
- Took a weekend vacation in Hawaii

Bad answers

- Sat at home and watched TV
- Went shopping
- Knitted some mittens

Interviewer: How do you spend your free time?

Good answers

- Coaching little league soccer
- Poking around old record shops in search of rare jazz albums
- Traveling to out-of-the-way places and then writing about them for the *New York Times*
- Playing the stock market

Bad answers

- Watching TV
- Hanging out with my friends in bars and getting wasted
- Picking up girls (or guys) before we get too wasted

Q&A Thought Balloons

Below are some examples of real questions job candidates have asked—and the thought balloons several interviewers confirm come close to being their own at times.

Candidate: I know your department is rated among the top three by I.I. (*Institutional Investor*) and is growing quickly in countries Y and Z in Asia. But both Y's and Z's currencies have recently been devalued, Z's obviously worse than Y's. How is this affecting your business here and overseas, and also your plans for the future in Y and Z?

Thought balloon: Better-than-average question. She understands one of our firm's core competencies and the most obvious way we differentiate ourselves from competitors. She's also a strong candidate to get sent to Asia in a few years given her claimed proficiency in Mandarin. Wonder if she's aware of the more serious cultural and political problems there . . . wonder how I can probe and find out how deeply she understands this?

Candidate: How long have you been at firm X and why? What do you like about the culture?

Thought balloon: Puff question. It is always easy to talk about myself. Should I mention how isolated I feel at times? Probably not. Need to reveal something, though, to make all the rest sound true.

Candidate: Could you walk me through your most recent day in the office?

Thought balloon: Typical but decent question—notwithstanding that she could have looked over a typical banker's day in WetFeet's *So, You Want to Be an Investment Banker*. Should I tell her about the sleeping-under-the-desk part?

Candidate: Your firm claims it's an "innovative, global" firm. Could you give me examples of things that are "innovative"?

Thought balloon: Hard to parse this one. This guy obviously reads the brochure babble. Is this some sophomoric attempt at scathing wit or does he really believe everything he reads? He looks earnest enough. But I really don't like that tiny earring. . . .

Candidate: One of the other bulge-bracket firms says your merger with X has diluted your strength in both Y and Z departments. Do you think that's true?

Thought balloon: A bit presumptuous, and I don't like her tattle-tale opener, but it's a valid question. One I'd want to know, too, before accepting an offer. I should probably admit both groups are "in play."

Candidate: How long, realistically, might it be before I actually begin trading/selling/meeting with clients?

Thought balloon: Legitimate question. He asked politely, and this is his job we're talking about. Problem is, of course, I have no idea. . . .

Examples of Good Questions to Ask Your Interviewer

- What sort of person seems to flourish at your firm long-term?
- If the firm is committed to becoming a more global player, what impact does that have on regional offices outside New York?
- After the training program is over, what is the process of assigning analysts and associates to industry groups?
- If you've worked on a project recently, could you describe what you liked best about it and what was most difficult?
- How are deals staffed?
- What do you think is the biggest challenge facing the firm in the next five years?

Questions to Avoid . . . and Their Dyspeptic Rejoinders

Candidate: I read in the paper that there is talk of a merger with another bank. Is this true? And if so, how will it affect jobs?

Thought balloon: (Inward sigh. Coupled with inward groan.) Heck, kid, everyone knows that no one knows the answer to the merger question, so why are you asking me this question? I wish people could come up with other ways of letting me know they read the paper.

Candidate: I have read that your Asia division may be doing a deal with a small China Sea oil company. Can you tell me more about it?

Thought balloon: Why are you asking me about Asia? You've expressed no interest in Asia until now. Nowhere on your resume does it say Asia. Don't you have questions about working here in the States? Some of us work too hard to worry about every detail of what is happening in the Asia group. I don't like questions that make me feel stupid.

Candidate: How long will it take me to make my first million?

Thought balloon: There have to be easier ways to earn a living at this bank. Maybe I could go work in IT, where no one seems to have an ego. This is ridiculous—you don't even have the job yet, pal.

Candidate: What differentiates your firm from the others?

Thought balloon: He's kidding, right? Here we are, almost lunchtime on Super Saturday. And he's asking me a question so dumb most people wouldn't dare ask it at a career fair. Too bad, he had promise.

A Student's Perspective

- Note to the Reader

- First and Foremost: Things You Should Know

- Getting the Interview

- Before the Interview

- At the Interview

- After the Interview

- Concluding Remarks

Note to the Reader

By now, you've read a few "how to ace your interview" guides (all of which I hope have helped). I'm willing to bet that all of those books were written by career experts. The front of this book certainly was. However, WetFeet is bringing you something more. Now that you know what the experts advise, read the following pages to get insight from someone who has been in exactly the position you're in now. I've gone through countless interviews and have plenty of stories about blunders and mistakes I made during some of those interviews. I try not to think about them, but you know what they say about learning from your mistakes? It's true! (See the Author's Bio for my success story.) And what's even better is learning from someone else's mistakes—i.e. mine—and figuring out what works without having to run your own experiments.

So by all means, use the expert advice that you've read and keep that in your back pocket. What I'll share are some of my personal experiences and strategies that I've found to be extremely effective in snagging a job in banking. Combine what you're about to read with what you've already read, and you'll be on your way.

First and Foremost: Things You Should Know

Know Yourself

Before you put yourself through the I-banking interview process, make sure you know who you are. Know what you want to do and why you want to do it. Understand that people get into investment banking for many reasons. This is a challenging career, and it's not the right path for everyone. Make sure you know what your motivations are. You'll be asked about them.

Think through and have responses in mind for all of these questions:

- Why do you want to be a banker?
- What activities have you done in the past?
- Where have you worked?
- What kind of person are you?
- What are your strengths and weaknesses?
- What do you love and hate?

Before you begin "reviewing," make sure you *know* yourself.

Every Firm, Interviewer, Interviewee, and Interview Is Different

Be sure to understand the differences among the firms, including their history, culture, and business. You know this already, right? Well, be aware that if you don't do your homework thoroughly, you may fall into traps without even knowing it.

For example: This past semester Goldman Sachs came to the University of Texas at Austin to recruit for its Dallas and Houston offices. On the day of the interviews, candidates were asked about their geographical preferences. A no-brainer, right? The answer's gotta be Houston or Dallas. However, it's not that simple. In Dallas, Goldman has two key divisions: wealth management and real estate. In Houston, however, Goldman has its investment banking division. I heard several candidates confidently say that they wanted to get into investment banking in Dallas. Clearly, they hadn't done their due diligence on the company. An immediate ding.

As you start interviewing, you'll notice differences in interviewing styles. The interview can be a pleasant experience when you meet with the types of bankers who are outgoing and enthusiastic. But then, there are those other types. Yes, we all know them: the ones who make their lives more interesting by making ours more stressful. You will no doubt be faced with the full spectrum—from easygoing to upsetting. Be prepared for them all.

Regardless of whom you meet, don't forget that the interviewer is not necessarily representative of the firm's culture. I've seen many students go sour on the firm they were interviewing with because they took a disliking to the interviewer. At any firm, you'll have your handful of the considerate and the cruel, so don't jump to conclusions—or close out your options—too quickly.

As for the interviews themselves, the types and lengths are manifold. You might have the standard 30-minute question-and-answer interview. Or you might have an interview that focuses on your behavior or personality, or an interview that is technically intense. The standard interview, which includes a mix of behavioral and technical questions, comprised about 80 percent of my interviews. The remaining interviews, however, were unique.

For example: At one bulge-bracket firm, the second-round interviewer focused solely on my life. More specifically, he asked questions about what I do for entertainment, my best spring break, and what I hate about investment banking. At another firm, I met with two stone-faced individuals—it was like speaking to a wall! At yet another, the interviewers introduced themselves and then asked me if I had any questions for the remaining 25 minutes. What it all boils down to is this: You don't know whom you're going to meet. So, be prepared to change gears at a moment's notice.

And finally, the content of your interview will also depend on your background. If you've interned or worked as an investment banker, you're more likely to get lobbed some technical questions. On the other hand, if you've never worked in banking before, be prepared to *prove* that investment banking is what you're passionate about.

Interviewing Is Often Subjective

At some point, you will walk out of an interview feeling confident because your gut tells you that you've nailed it—that phone call to invite you to the second round feels like a sure thing. But then, no phone call: you didn't make the cut. What happened? Interviews are subjective, and you can never really know what an interviewer is thinking. Of course, there are certain situations whose outcome may seem unfair to you. Life isn't always fair. Roll with the punches, and keep on moving.

For example: When I was interviewing for internships, I met with an interviewer from San Antonio, Texas. The interview candidate right before me was also from San Antonio. After the interviews, I spoke to the San Antonio candidate and asked him about his interview. As it turns out, all they talked about was San Antonio, the high schools they attended there, and so on. Nothing about the qualifications required for the job. Despite the fact that I'd felt good about my interview and was confident about getting a call back, it was the San Antonio candidate who was invited to the second round. An undeniable connection had been made, and I—the Houston native—was left out in the cold.

In another set of interviews with a bulge-bracket firm, I interviewed on campus and had friends who were also part of that interview round. Though many of us felt we had done well in our interviews, none of the 12 students on the interview schedule were selected for second rounds. So who was? The interviewer selected someone directly from his fraternity, a candidate who hadn't even been originally scheduled to interview. I was furious.

The point of these stories: You will do well in some interviews and still not get selected. Don't get discouraged; just be aware that the interview process can be and often is subjective.

Stress Levels Are High

Imagine a world in which you interviewed with your top firms, received several offers, and ultimately worked at the firm of your choice. Okay, fantasy aside, it's time to come back to reality. Through the booming 1990s, job seekers had the luxury of being able to pick and choose from a number of offers. Times have changed. Getting into I-banking is a serious challenge. If you want to break into the industry, get ready for skyrocketing stress levels as you take on more interviews than you think you can handle and struggle at keeping the words, "I quit," from entering your daily vocabulary.

My first internship—unpaid—was in Merrill Lynch's private client group. I landed my second internship with Enron after interviewing with 14 different companies, most of which were investment banks. Trust me, I didn't accept the Enron offer because I wanted to get a lesson in ethics, or the lack thereof; it was the only offer I received. The following year, I interviewed with more than

20 firms for another financial internship. Initially, I didn't get a single offer. Was I frustrated? Absolutely. Giving up was definitely a recurring thought, but I refused to give in to it.

With all that said, you should now know more about what to expect from this rigorous process. If banking is your life goal, know that you will travel a rough road while you're getting started—but many rewards lie ahead.

Getting the Interview

The Recruiting Shuffle

Now that you know what to expect, how do you go about getting an interview? The best way is to submit your resume through your university. Many banks recruit on campus and have resume submissions through various schools. You can also call firms directly.

Firms often recruit at universities that are located near the firm's operations. Most banks that recruit at the University of Texas at Austin, for example, are from the Houston area. The assumption is that because you're attending school in Texas, you want to stay in Texas; hence, firms recruit for positions within the state. However, occasionally firms recruit for other offices as well. That said, if you have a strong desire to work in New York, then you should contact the firm directly or get in touch with the recruiting coordinator.

Another effective method for landing an interview is to actively network. Read on for more about that.

Networking—What Is It, Why Do It, and How Do You Do It?

Networking is a term that comes up often, but what is it exactly? Ultimately, networking is about making connections through a number of routes both formal and informal. It involves interacting with people so that you can learn about them, their lines of work, their firms, and areas of growth in the industry. With effective networking you create a "people dictionary" of sorts, one in which you can look someone up and talk to them to learn more about what it is you're looking for and, most important, spot opportunities to pursue.

Consider this scenario: You're a VP of company XYZ, and you are responsible for making hiring decisions. Recently, you learned that the firm wants to hire another associate. You receive a stack of 100-plus resumes and have to select a handful. As you look over each resume for maybe 15 seconds, an old friend from high school gives you a call. She's looking for a job in banking and has kept in close contact with you for the past year. You know what she wants to do, that she's extremely capable, and has a great personality. So whom do you hire?

The qualified friend, of course. After all, why waste your firm's time and money in phone screening and flying out candidates for interviews, when you can bring in your friend whom you already know will hit it off with your coworkers, and make the hiring process quick, simple, and cost-effective. Put simply, most hiring managers give preference to friends or previous contacts. This is why you need to network.

Let me explain further. My internship hunt in the spring of 2002 was a frustrating experience. I thought I was well prepared for the recruiting process because I had completed an internship with Enron the previous summer. I received more than 20 interviews with many of the large bulge-bracket firms and some small boutique banks. But interview followed interview, and nothing came through. Even after several second-round interviews, I didn't get a single offer.

Suddenly, one phone call changed everything. Someone I'd met while I was a resident assistant at my university dormitory got in touch with me along with a few others when he learned that Deutsche Bank in San Francisco was looking for a summer intern. (Earlier that fall, this contact—whom I got to know during dorm meetings and occasionally played basketball with—had received an offer from Deutsche to join its technology group.) After two phone interviews, the firm flew me to San Francisco. After six interviews, I received an internship offer. This experience convinced me of the impact of—in this case, informal—networking.

So how do you network? Start with people you already know. Make a list of anyone in the industry you can talk to. Whatever you do, keep in mind that you should *never* ask for an interview or a job. Your aim should be information gathering. Let's assume, for example, that one of your friend's parents works at a bank. Make a phone call to express your interest in gaining insight into the industry. Find out exactly what your friend's parent does. Ask questions to find out what he or she loves and hates about the job. Ask about the role of an investment banker at that specific firm. Learn as much as you can.

Once you've got the ball rolling, expand your network. Look through an alumni database at your university. Call friends you know who are working in the industry. Get in touch with classmates and anyone else who can help you gather information.

In the spring of 2001, I interviewed with a representative at Goldman Sachs for the sales and trading division. Though I wasn't invited to second rounds, I held on to my interviewer's business card, keeping in mind that she worked in the San Francisco office. The following year when I worked at Deutsche Bank in San Francisco, I sent her an e-mail to let her know that I was in the area and that I was still interested in learning more about Goldman Sachs. She was shocked; she didn't expect someone who'd interviewed with her a year ago to contact her. We spoke over the phone, and she invited me for lunch and later gave me a tour of the trading desk. Wait, how did this happen? That's right: networking. My interaction with her helped me more than I could have imagined. As she continued to guide and advise me on my career decisions, she became my mentor. She also helped me get an interview with the investment banking division, and although it did not lead to an offer, I learned a great deal more about the industry. Most important, I found an amazing mentor.

Before the Interview

Soaking It All Up

Before you get to the interview, recall the three Rs of interview preparation: research, rehearse, and review. I rarely used all of the data that I'd prepared for my interviews. Finance issues, banking, and past work experiences didn't always come up. You never know just what you'll be asked—as I've said before, every interview is different. So prepare for any potential angle an interviewer may present to you.

Don't stop at researching the firms that are interviewing you or the industry in general. Get to know their competitors' firms, too. Be prepared to explain why you prefer investment baking to consulting, for example. Research markets, equities, current industry events, and more.

Then be sure to rehearse and review the information you've gathered. Develop a point of view among all this data. Make sure you understand it fully. Conduct mock interviews with your friends to start formulating responses to potential questions and delivering those responses smoothly and confidently. Once you've completed the three Rs, you're all set for the interview.

Sample Interview Questions

Throughout my interview rounds, I answered many of the same questions. However, I've also had my share of less-than-traditional questions—ranging from the very technical to very bizarre. Look over the list below to get a feel for the most common types of questions you can expect. Make sure you have a solid and thorough answer for each.

- Can you tell me about yourself?
- Why do you want to work in banking?
- What does an investment banker do?
- What do you enjoy outside of school?
- Tell me something about yourself that is not on your resume.
- Why did you choose to attend this school?
- Why do you want to work at our firm?
- What are your strengths and weaknesses?
- Whom else are you interviewing with?
- What would your friends say about you?

Avoiding Silly Mistakes

People often make mistakes without even realizing they've done so. There are several pitfalls to avoid. First, know the position and location you are applying for. For example, most banks are strategically located: Technology groups are usually in the San Francisco area, energy groups are in Houston, generalists are in New York, and so on. So if you are passionate about technology banking, it doesn't make sense to tell your interviewer you want to work in technology but reside in Houston.

I've said it before, but it bears repeating: Know the bank you're interviewing with. At a Lehman interview, I was discussing trends in investment banking. At that time, many commercial and investment banks were merging. During one interview, I began talking about the strategy behind such mergers. The interviewer then asked if I thought the merging of commercial and investment banks was the best strategy. Knowing that Lehman's strategy was to remain as an investment bank, I was instantly on alert. I knew I had to tread carefully and temper my response with this knowledge. Expounding on the virtues of merging without this understanding would have demonstrated my lack of knowledge of the company.

At the Interview

The Judges' Scorecard Part II

So what do the interviewers look for? That's a tough question, especially when you consider what I've already discussed. But there are consistent qualities interviewers agree on across the board: enthusiasm and a willingness to work hard. It's up to you to show them how excited you are about the firm and how well you fit within the culture. Think about what you would look for if you were hiring someone, or better yet, the kind of person you would want to work with. Probably someone who has focus, takes initiative, works well with teams, and whom you can get along with on a daily basis. Remember the Airplane Test mentioned previously, and make sure you pass that, too!

We have discussed one of the judges, the interviewer, but people tend to neglect the other: you. Don't forget that you are also interviewing the firm at the same time the firm is interviewing you. Your goal is to find out as much as possible about where you'll be working, whom you'll be working with, what you'll be doing, and so on. Remember, you are about to commit to an analyst or associate program that could affect the course of your life for several years. You want to enjoy your experience as much as possible and ensure that it's a good fit for your future goals.

The Introduction

When you walk into the interview room, you'll probably have millions of thoughts racing through your head. Let them go. Even after having several interviews under my belt, I always found myself getting tense. I dreaded shaking hands as my palms would always get sweaty. Eventually, I started keeping a napkin in my pocket; I would put my hand in my pocket and wipe my hand right before I had to shake hands. That's where it starts after all—a nice, firm, and preferably dry handshake. Look back at the "Favorite Interview Gaffes" and "Body Language Dos and Don'ts" to review how to make a great first impression.

My suggestion is to walk in, shake hands, smile, and ask the interviewer how he or she is doing. I frequently started with a greeting such as, "It must be nice to get a break from the office for a day." This opener almost always broke the ice and started the interview on the right foot. Your icebreaker is critical; it sets the tone for the rest of the interview—and a conversational interview is your goal.

Initially, most interviewers will introduce themselves and then ask you to tell them about yourself. This is an opportunity for you to go over your life in 60 seconds. Throughout the interview process, your aim is to make the stranger on the other side of the table like you. We could get into the whole psychology of interviewing, but let's keep it simple: If you are trying to make a friend who can push you to the next round, you need to find something you have in common with that person. Your mission is to form a bond so that he or she remembers you. When interviewers asked me about myself, I would walk them through my educational and work experiences. I always mentioned the time I studied abroad in London, saying something like: "In the summer of 2000, I went abroad to London and took a course in valuation and entrepreneurship. Outside of school, I met Tom Cruise and Angelina Jolie at the premier of *Mission Impossible II* and watched Pete Sampras at Wimbledon."

With that, I was hoping to somehow connect with my interviewer on one or more fronts. I was hoping he or she had either worked or studied abroad, enjoyed movies, or was a sports fan. In fact, this bit of information often led to discussions about sports, movies, or London. In two of my interviews, all we discussed was my time abroad. Not only had I managed to successfully connect with my interviewer so that he or she would remember me, but I'd effectively conveyed that I had the kind of dynamic personality that would complement the firm and its working environment.

Getting to Know Your Interviewer—and Using that to Your Advantage

After the introduction, you need to quickly size up your interviewer's style and personality. Once you've assessed his or her style, you can match your interviewing style accordingly. For example, if you're meeting with someone who is relaxed and easygoing, it might be okay to discuss some of your activities that are not directly related to banking. You might want to use light humor if the opportunity arises. On the other hand, if you're meeting with a more serious person, then you may choose a style that is concise and straightforward, discussing only experiences that are relevant to banking.

I have found that many of my best interviews moved away from traditional interview styles to one that was more of a dialogue. The interviews that assumed a conversational tone were often more interesting and yielded better results. One effective way to start a dialogue is to follow one of your answers with an appropriate question.

For example: In an interview with Wachovia Securities, the interviewer described an ethical dilemma he had recently encountered. He then asked what I would do in such a situation. I first asked a couple of questions to make sure I understood the situation correctly and then responded. Following my answer, I immediately asked him how he'd handled the situation. He responded, and from there, we began talking about ethical dilemmas in the workplace and how to handle them. Once our dialogue got rolling, a rapport was established.

Another effective strategy is to show the interviewer you're a good listener. Sounds simple, right? Well, it's not always that easy when you're under the gun, trying to impress. Have you ever sat through an interview, asked questions, and then forgotten everything your interviewer just told you? Make an effort to listen and remember. Demonstrating an attention to detail and an understanding of what a particular firm is all about can only increase your chances of making it to the next round.

For example: Let's say you are at your 15th information session, and despite your boredom you decide to pay close attention. Jim has come in to speak and will be conducting interviews tomorrow. Jim is from XYZ Bank and emphasizes how his firm gives its associates and analysts substantial responsibility. The next day, you interview with Jim, and now it's time for you to ask questions. You say: "Jim, yesterday at the information session you stressed how your firm gives substantial responsibility to employees. Can you describe a recent transaction that you worked on and the responsibility you gave to the analyst?"

In this scenario, you've managed to score several key points. First, you've displayed that you cared enough to attend the information session. Second, you've proved that you listen carefully. Finally, you've demonstrated a genuine interest in the position by asking for a specific example. Add all of this to that the fact that you will gain valuable insight into whether you'll be building financial models or making copies—a key bit of data in deciding whether the job is the right one for you later on, when you're considering the offer.

Here's another example: Let's say you are interviewing with Bob from ABC Bank, and in his introduction he tells you he worked at XYZ Bank and LMN

Bank before ending up at ABC Bank. At the end of the interview, Bob asks if you have any questions. You say: "Bob, you mentioned that you moved from XYZ Bank to LMN Bank before you arrived at ABC Bank. I'm curious as to why you chose ABC Bank and what is it specifically about the firm that keeps you there?"

In this scenario, you've shown that you were paying close attention to Bob when he introduced himself. You have also demonstrated to Bob that you really do care about the firm you will go to work for. In addition, Bob gets to talk about his path in banking as well as the merits of his firm—two topics most bankers love to talk about.

To recap, you have 30 minutes to make a friend, convince your interviewer that you are passionate about being an investment banker, and get yourself invited to second rounds or, better yet, an offer. And those 30 minutes could determine your summer or the next several years, so use the discussed strategies to get the job you want.

Concluding Your Interview

When you come to the end of your interview, ask several questions to gather more information. Keep in mind the time. If it's a 30-minute interview and there's one minute remaining, ask one quick question. If you've got 15 minutes left, you probably have time for more involved questions. Review the "Sample Interview Questions" covered previously.

Be sure to say thank you, smile, and ask for a business card. Even if you don't make the second round this time, you'd be wise to hold onto your interviewer's card and add the interviewer to your network.

After the Interview

Thank-You E-Mails Can't Hurt

Thank-you e-mails definitely can't hurt (unless they include a grammar or spelling mistake). Of course, I've known people who've received job offers without having sent a thank-you e-mail, and it's likely that the e-mail will get shoved right into the recycle bin. But it's a good way of demonstrating your courtesy, professionalism, and interest in the position.

Receiving Offers and Declines

Now that the interviews are finally over, you're desperately waiting for the phone call. I know how it feels to be in this post-interview limbo. I also know—all too well—how it feels when you don't get an offer. Let's assume, however, that you do receive an offer. Under no circumstances should you accept on the spot unless you are 100 percent sure. Of course, some will expect you to accept immediately. For example, I once received a call from a managing director, who said, "We want to extend you an offer," and then paused. It was as if he expected me to accept right then and there.

Some firms gave me as little as one week to make my decision, while others offered as much as two months' time to think over the offer. Ideally, we want all of our offers on the table at once so that we can pick the best of the bunch. Unfortunately, the timing rarely works out so neatly. On the flip side, consider the recruiters' perspectives. If a firm interviews five candidates in the final round and needs to hire one person, an offer will be made immediately.

However, the firm can't afford to give that person months to make a decision because the other candidates are also waiting to hear back.

Then there's the bad news, which usually goes like this: "Hey, how are you? Great. I'm glad everything is going well. We really enjoyed meeting with you, and we're glad you showed interest in our firm. [Here it comes.] Unfortunately, we are unable to extend an offer to you at this time. Thank you for your interest and good luck."

Yes, I hate this phone call just as much as the next person does. All you can do is listen, feel your stomach start to ache, and say thank you. You never know; you may run into your interviewer in the future. Keep in mind that declines aren't always bad. Hold onto your interviewer's business card and make contact occasionally. Remember that every interview is an opportunity to develop and maintain a positive relationship and add to your network, even if you don't get the offer.

Concluding Remarks

Now that you've read through this section, I hope you are feeling more confident and better prepared for the interviews. You know what the experts have said, and now you have new insight based on real interviewing experiences from someone in the trenches. Keep in mind that we don't live in a perfect world, so you should anticipate making mistakes when you begin the process. However, the key is to learn from your mistakes. As you make your journey through the interview process, let what you've read and your own experiences enrich your approach to the interviews so that you eventually land the investment banking job of your dreams.

Student Perspective Author Bio

Vivek Shah, a Houston native, is a recent graduate from the McCombs School of Business (University of Texas at Austin) where he majored in business honors and finance. At the university, Vivek was active in several organizations. He served as a peer career advisor, working closely with students to advise them on the recruiting process. He was part of the founding class of Delta Sigma Pi, a co-ed professional business fraternity, and later served as its vice president. Vivek also served on an evaluation committee for the Mitte Business Honors Program.

Before attending McCombs, Vivek worked at Merrill Lynch in the private client services division. He later attended the London School of Economics and Political Science where he took advanced courses on valuation and entrepreneurship. Vivek worked as a consultant to PromoOrder.com in Austin. In addition, he interned at Enron with the natural gas group, where he gained valuable experience in energy trading and research. More recently, Vivek worked at Deutsche Bank in its technology group in San Francisco.

Vivek received five full-time offers from Lehman Brothers, Deutsche Bank, Wachovia Securities, and others. He has accepted a full-time job with Simmons & Company International, an energy investment bank in Houston. He recently cofounded a non-profit business consulting company.

WETFEET'S INSIDER GUIDE SERIES

JOB SEARCH GUIDES

Getting Your Ideal Internship

Job Hunting A to Z: Landing the Job You Want

Killer Consulting Resumes!

Killer Investment Banking Resumes!

Killer Cover Letters & Resumes!

Negotiating Your Salary & Perks

Networking Works!

INTERVIEW GUIDES

Ace Your Case: Consulting Interviews

Ace Your Case II: 15 More Consulting Cases

Ace Your Case III: Practice Makes Perfect

Ace Your Case IV: The Latest & Greatest

Ace Your Case V: Return to the Case Interview

Ace Your Interview!

Beat the Street: Investment Banking Interviews

Beat the Street II: I-Banking Interview Practice Guide

CAREER & INDUSTRY GUIDES

Careers in Accounting

Careers in Advertising & Public Relations

Careers in Asset Management & Retail Brokerage

Careers in Biotech & Pharmaceuticals

Careers in Brand Management

Careers in Consumer Products

Careers in Entertainment & Sports

Careers in Human Resources

Careers in Information Technology

Careers in Investment Banking

Careers in Management Consulting

Careers in Manufacturing

Careers in Marketing & Market Research

Careers in Nonprofits & Government Agencies

Careers in Real Estate

Careers in Supply Chain Management

Careers in Venture Capital

Consulting for PhDs, Doctors & Lawyers

Industries & Careers for MBAs

Industries & Careers for Undergrads

COMPANY GUIDES

Accenture

Bain & Company

Boston Consulting Group

Booz Allen Hamilton

Citigroup's Corporate & Investment Bank

Credit Suisse First Boston

Deloitte Consulting

Goldman Sachs Group

J.P. Morgan Chase & Company

Lehman Brothers

McKinsey & Company

Merrill Lynch

Morgan Stanley

25 Top Consulting Firms

Top 20 Biotechnology & Pharmaceuticals Firms

Top 25 Financial Services Firms